Beginning Machine Learning in the Browser

Quick-start Guide to Gait Analysis with JavaScript and TensorFlow.js

Nagender Kumar Suryadevara

Apress®

Beginning Machine Learning in the Browser: Quick-start Guide to Gait Analysis with JavaScript and TensorFlow.js

Nagender Kumar Suryadevara
School of Computer and Information Sciences,
University of Hyderabad, Hyderabad, Telangana, India

ISBN-13 (pbk): 978-1-4842-6842-1
https://doi.org/10.1007/978-1-4842-6843-8

ISBN-13 (electronic): 978-1-4842-6843-8

Managing Director, Apress Media LLC: Welmoed Spahr
Acquisitions Editor: Aaron Black
Development Editor: James Markham
Coordinating Editor: Jessica Vakili

Distributed to the book trade worldwide by Springer Science+Business Media New York, 1 NY Plazar, New York, NY 10014. Phone 1-800-SPRINGER, fax (201) 348-4505, e-mail orders-ny@springer-sbm.com, or visit www.springeronline.com. Apress Media, LLC is a California LLC and the sole member (owner) is Springer Science + Business Media Finance Inc (SSBM Finance Inc). SSBM Finance Inc is a Delaware corporation.

For information on translations, please e-mail booktranslations@springernature.com; for reprint, paperback, or audio rights, please e-mail bookpermissions@springernature.com.

Apress titles may be purchased in bulk for academic, corporate, or promotional use. eBook versions and licenses are also available for most titles. For more information, reference our Print and eBook Bulk Sales web page at http://www.apress.com/bulk-sales.

Any source code or other supplementary material referenced by the author in this book is available to readers on GitHub via the book's product page, located at www.apress.com/978-1-4842-6842-1. For more detailed information, please visit http://www.apress.com/source-code.

Printed on acid-free paper

Table of Contents

About the Author

Dr. Nagender Kumar Suryadevara received his Ph.D. degree from the School of Engineering and Advanced Technology, Massey University, New Zealand, in 2014. He is an Associate Professor at the School of Computer and Information Sciences, University of Hyderabad, India. His research interests include wireless sensor networks, the Internet of Things, and time-series data mining. He has authored two books, edited two books, and published more than 50 papers in various international journals, conferences, and book chapters. He has delivered numerous presentations, including keynote, tutorial, and special lectures. He is a senior member of IEEE. Dr. Suryadevara is passionate about development possibilities for great AI-based products in resource-constrained computing environments. Google Scholar citations:h-index:19,i10-index:30.

https://scholar.google.com/citations?user=S28OdGMAAAAJ&hl=en

About the Technical Reviewer

Vishwesh Ravi Shrimali graduated from BITS Pilani, where he studied mechanical engineering, in 2018. Since then, he has worked with BigVision LLC on deep learning and computer vision and was involved in creating official OpenCV AI courses. Currently, he is working at Mercedes Benz Research and Development India Pvt. Ltd. He has a keen interest in programming and AI and has applied that interest in mechanical engineering projects. He has also written multiple blogs on OpenCV and deep learning on LearnOpenCV, a leading blog on computer vision. He has also authored *Machine Learning for OpenCV* (2nd edition) by Packt. When he is not writing blogs or working on projects, he likes to go on long walks or play his acoustic guitar.

Acknowledgments

This journey would not have been possible without the support of my family, professors, mentors, and friends. I am especially grateful to my parents, who supported me emotionally. To my family, thank you for encouraging me in all of my pursuits and inspiring me to follow my dreams.

I want to express my sincere gratitude and heartfelt thanks to **Vishwesh Ravi Shrimali** for allocating some time and taking responsibility for reviewing the book chapters and providing valuable comments and helpful suggestions.

Thanks to everyone in the publication team, especially **Aaron Black**, who helped me in getting the book content into great shape, **James Markham**, who took great pains in grooming the book, and **Jessica Vakili,** who made sure the book writing process went smoothly and on time.

I am indebted to many of my students and colleagues who were involved with various projects over several years, and some of their works have been used in this book. I would especially like to give credit to one of my students, Ashish Gupta, for helping me in executing the programs in Chapter 5.

Preface

In recent times, artificial intelligence (AI) and machine learning (ML) techniques have been widely used in many applications, such as monitoring environmental parameters, monitoring, and control of industrial situations, intelligent transportation, structural health monitoring, health care, and so on. The advancement of electronics, embedded control, smart sensing, networking, and communication has made it possible to develop low-cost smart systems. Although there are smart systems, the computing capabilities are minimal, and hence they are considered to be resource-constrained computing devices (e.g., mobile phones, smart watches, and mini electronic gadgets).

Applying smart strategies involving complex mathematical operations of AI and ML methods on resource-constrained computing devices and browsers is challenging. The advancements in Internet technologies, primarily JavaScript skills, have made it possible to execute AI/ML models in the browsers and resource computing devices. There are many other publications on AI, ML, and JavaScript, but this book provides beneficial information and practical knowledge to develop intelligent methods/models from scratch and deploy them on browsers and resource-constrained computing devices.

The complete book is divided into six chapters:

Chapter 1 describes the fundamentals of web development. This chapter provides a short description of designing and developing web applications using web building blocks. For developing an AI/ML model and running on the browser or resource-constrained computing device, this chapter's practical knowledge is essential. For a beginner in any field of study and interested in developing web apps, this chapter provides the necessary practical skills to better realize web applications.

Chapter 2 delivers the steps to be performed and the necessary JavaScript libraries to be considered for processing the data at the computer's browser application level. The latest JavaScript libraries (p5.js and ml5.js) that help build the AI/ML models with practical steps are covered.

Chapter 3 introduces the human pose estimation application as an example that enables the reader to understand how an AI/ML model involving complex mathematical operations can be used to run in the browser. The stepwise procedure teaches you how to implement ML methods to estimate an individual's poses.

Chapter 4 covers the open-source JavaScript library TensorFlow. js, which will be useful for building and deploying AI/ML models in the browser. The architecture of the TensorFlow.js, including its accelerators that support massive data processing at the browser, is explained. Practical examples of executing a neural network model for useful classification tasks are elucidated using the TensorFlow.js library.

Chapter 5 examines how to determine gait parameters by applying AI/ML methods along with the JavaScript libraries in the web browser application. The chapter walks you through the basics of gait analysis and expands on the observational method considered in determining the vital parameters for analysis using the AI in the browser.

Chapter 6 provides a few more advanced applications to run on the browser by applying the AI/ML methods. This chapter encourages the reader to think about the advancements possible when running AI/ML models in the browser.

I hope that you enjoy reading the book. If you need any help whatsoever with the practicals, please feel free to contact me.

Dr. S. Nagender Kumar Suryadevara

Associate Professor, School of Computer and Information Sciences, University of Hyderabad, India.

CHAPTER 1

Web Development

This chapter introduces you to the fundamentals of machine learning (ML) and provides a practical primer to web design and development for complete beginners. Topics covered in this chapter include the following:

- Hypertext Markup Language (HTML)
- Cascading Style Sheets (CSS)
- JavaScript (JS)
- Document Object Model (DOM)
- jQuery

These building blocks of web development enable you to implement rich user functionalities into your web design.

Machine Learning Overview

Machine learning, a subset of artificial intelligence (AI), aims to enable computers to learn without interacting with specific programs. ML enables computers to develop programs that can access data and use it to learn for themselves (and thus perform like a human).

© Nagender Kumar Suryadevara 2021
N. K. Suryadevara, *Beginning Machine Learning in the Browser*,
https://doi.org/10.1007/978-1-4842-6843-8_1

Arthur Samuel, who believed that computers could learn without specific programs, popularized the term *machine learning* in 1959. In 1997, Tom Mitchell further clarified the concept of ML, stating that a computer could learn from some relative measure involving past performance while processing some task, thus giving some *experience* to the computer.

Today, electronics of all kinds are outfitted with cutting-edge, high-sensitivity sensors. Further, Internet connectivity allows for communication among gadgets (things) for better environment-condition monitoring. Accordingly, the massive amount of data generated from these gadgets drives the Internet of Things (IoT) concept. Using AI and ML strategies, the broad information gathered can be processed, scaled, ordered, and used to predict events.

In conventional ML approaches, data is sent to and handled through a central server, which experiences communication overhead, latency, protection loss, and security issues. To overcome these difficulties, inferences from the data collected in the IoT realm can be made by deploying better ML techniques near the data origin using, for instance, browser-environment capabilities. Exploiting ML strategies on resource-constrained computing devices through a browser helps respective entities to make better decisions in real time for enhanced functionality.

The tremendous computational demands of current AI strategies and the development of ever-increasing numbers of AI-enhanced applications forecast more data-processing problems. After all, computer-based intelligence systems features are more demanding as they seek to reduce resource utilization, to quicken resource accessibility, and to exploit resource utilization for precision.

Software developers and engineers can now more effectively leverage AI to conceptualize exceptionally responsive applications that respond to user-sourced information in real time, such as voice or facial recognition. They can also make smarter applications that can learn from user behavior.

Computer-based intelligence enables us to automate applications to incorporate substantive proposals, to respond to voice requests or physical motions, to use mobile phone cameras to recognize items or places, and to figure out how to help users with day-by-day activities.

In the past, many of the best ML and deep learning (DL) systems required familiarity with Python and its related library system. Production of ML models required unique reasoning equipment and programming tools, such as NVIDIA graphical processing units (GPUs) and CUDA. Now, however, incorporating ML into JavaScript (JS) applications often involves deploying the ML part on remote cloud systems, such as Amazon Web Services (AWS), and getting the model to run on the local system via application programming interface (API) calls. This nonlocal, back-end centered methodology has likely kept many web engineers from taking advantage of the abundant prospects AI offers to front-end improvement.

The main advantage of running AI strategies on users' local devices (i.e., near the data-origin source) is that the information never leaves the user's device. This point is critically significant because users rightfully worry about their data privacy, especially in the wake of well-publicized and embarrassing information leaks and security breaches.

With the help of TensorFlow.js software tools, developers/users can exploit AI without sending their information over a system that potentially makes it available to an outsider. These tools make it simpler to develop secure applications that comply with information security guidelines, such as healthcare applications that read wearable clinical sensors. The tools also make AI program augmentation possible, thus allowing upgrades while shielding user conduct/information.

Integrating JS programming features with AI strategies in a simple interface can lead to more straightforward access to rich sensor information from IoT devices. User behavior can be modeled based on interactivity with device information sources such as voice or webcams. Because similar programming code can run on, for example, mobile phones utilizing accelerometers, gyroscopes, and Global Positioning System (GPS), integrating AI computational capabilities into user devices themselves can prove highly beneficial.

Web Communication

Figure 1-1 shows the big-picture web basics for AI applications that run on user devices.

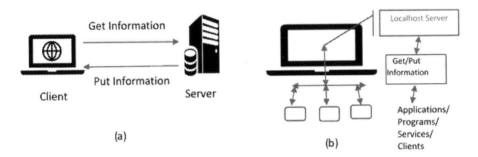

Figure 1-1. *Web communication through the Internet and localhost*

The three web development essentials are as follows:

- Client (web browsers, used to surf the web)
- Server systems (used to supply information to the browsers)
- Computer networks (used to support browser-server communication)

The web activity shown in Figure 1-1(a) illustrates the internetworking principle, where communication between the client and server is done through protocols such as the Internet Protocol (IP), Transmission Control Protocol (TCP), Hypertext Transfer Protocol (HTTP), and the File Transfer Protocol (FTP). Figure 1-1(b) shows that communication between the client (browser/services/applications) and the server (localhost) happens locally and provides the required information to the respective applications (client/browser/services).

The following terms relate to the communication:

- *World Wide Web (WWW or web)*: A system of interlinked, hypertext documents that runs over the Internet. There are two types of software: client and server. A system that wants to access the information provided by servers must run client software (e.g., a web browser), and an Internet-connected computer that wants to provide information to others must run server software. The client and server applications communicate over the Internet by following a protocol built on TCP/IP (i.e., HTTP) (Figure 1-2).

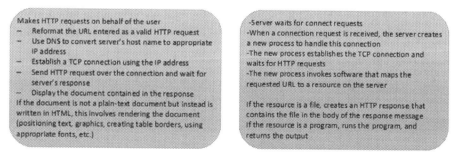

Figure 1-2. *The communication between the web client (browser) and the web server*

- *Hypertext*: An information format that enables one to move from one part of a document to another or from one document to another through hyperlinks.

- *Uniform Resource Locator (URL)*: Unique identifiers used to locate a particular resource on the network.

- *Markup language*: Defines the structure and content of hypertext documents.

Organizing the Web with HTML

To design and develop web pages, you want to be thoroughly familiar with Hypertext Markup Language (HTML). HTML enables you to define a web page's structure, including sections, lists, headings, connection points, pictures, mixed-media players, and more.

HTML is not a programming language. It is a markup language that tells Internet browsers how to structure web pages that a user visits. HTML consists of various components that you use to manipulate substantive page elements to show in a specific way. Encasing labels, for instance, can turn content into a hyperlink that associates with another page or can be used to emphasize words/terms.

Web Development Using IDEs/Editors

The difference between an integrated development environment (IDE) and an editor (text) for web development is that an IDE does everything from fundamental content management to advanced development that cannot be done with a text editor.

For example, editors such as ***Sublime, Notepad++,*** and ***Atom*** can be used with HTML and Cascading Style Sheets (CSS) when writing the code for web page design. These editors include many good features (e.g., language structures that include adaptable interfaces and comprehensive navigation tools for web developers who want enhanced application capabilities).

For instance, a web developer may require a debugger and a compiler to develop web applications effectively. Figure 1-3 shows the programming environments of these three editors.

Figure 1-3. *Notepad++, Sublime, and Atom editor environments*

With the best IDEs, however, you have less to worry about. They often include comprehensive development tools in one application, including for automation, testing, and forecasting. Mainly, they provide web developers the necessary support to transform code into a working application. Here are some of the more popular IDEs:

- *Visual Studio Code*: Visual Studio Code is perhaps the best JavaScript IDE for Windows, Mac, and Linux platforms. In addition to supporting JS functionality, it also supports Node.js and TypeScript features, and it includes a system of extensions for different programming dialects, including C++, C#, Python, and PHP. Visual Studio Code makes for programmer-friendly operations with excellent syntax features and autocomplete with IntelliSense that responds to myriad factors, word definitions, and imported modules.

- *NetBeans*: NetBeans is one of the best web development IDEs because it enables you to create a neat and versatile work area and develop web applications quickly. It also works well with JS, HTML5, PHP, and C/C++. It is a free JS IDE and a great HTML5 IDE for everyday use. This IDE allows you to review code for errors and lets you automatically fix syntax if necessary (including for Java 8 features such as lambda expressions).

- *PyCharm*: PyCharm is not the best free JS IDE. However, the paid Professional Edition is worth considering if you are looking for a solid web development IDE for Python.

- *IntelliJ IDEA*: IntelliJ IDEA is an excellent web development IDE. A free version is available, but if you want all the JS features it offers, consider the paid Ultimate Edition. IntelliJ IDEA can save you time and energy in web development, and it is an excellent CSS IDE. Note, as well, that it supports a wide range of programming dialects.

Building Blocks of Web Development

The three building blocks of web development are as follows:

- *HTML*: Via HTML5, computers can now understand what is on your website rather than just display website content dynamically. Earlier HTML versions provide static or dynamic information to the users. Website content is shown via HTML code.

- *CSS*: CSS determines what the website/pages look like. HTML is for making the content, whereas CSS is for showing the content in the way you want (i.e., the design; the different styles, colors, backgrounds, and layout). CSS makes a website/page look interesting.

- *JavaScript*: JS is a programming language used to manipulate HTML and CSS. Its main function is to provide interactive features for the user. It is sturdy and can be used to create full web applications (apps).

Note   To develop and test the applications/code in this book, consider using Google's Chrome browser, which has versions for Mac, Windows, and Linux.

HTML and CSS Programming

A coherent web development process requires that you first define *what* you want to say (HTML) and then define *how* you want to say it (CSS). An HTML component (element) is the combination of a start tag, its characteristics (attributes), an end tag, and everything in between.

An HTML tag—either opening (< >) or closing (</ >)—is used to identify the beginning or end of a component (element). The following code shows the structure of an HTML document and some of its basic elements:

```
<!DOCTYPE html>
<html>
  <head>
    <!-- Metadata goes here -->
  </head>
  <body>
    <!-- Content goes here -->
  </body>
</html>
```

The first line, `<!DOCTYPE html>`, informs the browser that it is an HTML5 version web page. The entire web page content is to be wrapped in `<html>` tags. The actual `<html>` text is called an *opening tag*, and `</html>` is called a *closing tag*. Everything inside of these tags is considered part of the `<html>` *element*, which is the actual thing that gets created when a web browser parses your HTML tags. Inside the `<html>` element are two more elements: `<head>` and `<body>`. A web page `<head>` contains all of its metadata, such as the page title, any CSS style sheets, and other things required to render the page but that you do not necessarily want the user to see. The bulk of our HTML markup will live in the `<body>` element, which represents the visible content of the page.

Comments are given between the tags `<!--` and `-->`. Listing 1-1 shows a more complete HTML example, and Figure 1-4 shows the corresponding output.

Listing 1-1. Basic HTML Content of a Web Page

```
<html>
<head>
<title>
Basic HTML Web Page
</title>
</head>
<body>
<h1> Web Development is Easy! </h1>
<p> First, we need to learn some basic HTML </p>
<h2> Headings </h2>
<p> Headings structure the outline of the website.
There are six levels of headings </p>
<h2> Lists </h2>
<p> There are two types of Lists </p>
<h3> Unordered List </h3>
<ul>
 <li>Add a "ul" element (it stands for unordered list)</li>
 <li>Add each item in its own "li" element</li>
 <li>They don't need to be in any particular order</li>
</ul>
<h3> Ordered List </h3>
<ol>
  <li>Notice the new "ol" element wrapping everything</li>
  <li>But, the list item elements are the same</li>
  <li>Also note how the numbers increment on their own</li>
  <li>You should be noticing things is this precise order,
because this is an ordered list</li>
</ol>
<h2>Inline Elements</h2>
```

```
<p><em>Sometimes</em>, you need to draw attention to a
particular word or
phrase.</p>
<p>This is some <em>emphasized text</p></em>
<p>Other times you need to <strong>strong</strong>ly emphasize
the importance of a word or phrase.</p>
<h2>Empty Elements and Line break using br tag</h2>
<p>Web Programming is easier.</p>
<p>Regards,<br/>
The Authors</p>
<h2> Horizontal Line </h2>
<hr/>
<p>P.S. This is a basic HTML Web page to understand how a web
page looks like. </p>
</body>
</html>
```

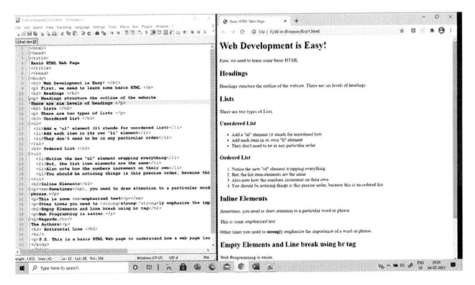

Figure 1-4. *Screenshot of the basic HTML code and its output*

Dynamic HTML

Dynamic HTML (DHTML) enables developers to control the display and position of HTML elements in a browser window. HTML is used to create static web pages, and DHTML is used to create dynamic web pages. HTML consists of simple HTML tags, whereas DHTML consists of HTML tags plus CSS plus JS.

Cascading Style Sheets

CSS helps us to specify how elements on the web page should be presented. With CSS, we can determine the style and layout of the web page. There are three ways to use style sheets:

- Inline style sheets (Listing 1-2)

- Embedded style sheets (Listing 1-3)

- External style sheets (Listing 1-4)

Inline Style Sheets

An inline style sheet is used to apply various unique styles to a single element. You can also use an inline style sheet to define a style for a special type of element or add a class attribute to the element. Listing 1-2 shows how inline styles can be used along with HTML elements. Figure 1-5 shows the corresponding output.

Listing 1-2. Inline Style Sheets Example

```
<HTML>
<head>
<TITLE> Inline Style sheets </TITLE>
</head>
<Body>
<p> This is Simple Text </p>
<p Style="font-size:30pt; font-family:arial"> This text is
different </p>
<p style="font-size:40pt;color:#ff0000"> This text is colored
</p>
</Body>
</HTML>
```

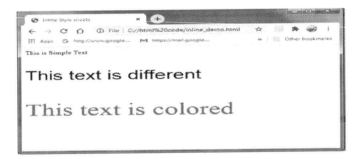

Figure 1-5. *Output of the inline CSS style settings*

Embedded Style Sheets

For embedded style sheets, we write all desired selectors along with the properties and values in the head section. Then, in the body section, newly defined selector tags are used with the actual content. The DHTML script in Listing 1-3 defines h1, h2, h3, and p selectors with different properties and values. Figure 1-6 shows the corresponding output of the embedded style settings along with the HTML code.

Note that to define embedded style sheets we have to mention style type= "test/css" in the head section.

Listing 1-3. Embedded Style Sheets Example

```
<HTML>
<head>
<TITLE> Embedded Style sheets </TITLE>
<style type="text/css">
h1,h2,h3{font-family:arial;}
h2 {color:red;left:20px }
h3 {color:blue;}
p {font-size:14pt;font-family:verdana;}
.special {color:green}
</style>
</head>
<Body>
<h1 class="special"> <center>
This page is created using Embedded style sheets </center> </h1>
<h2> This line is aligned left and red colored </h2>
<p> The embedded style sheet is the most commonly used style
sheet. This paragraph is written in Verdana font with font size
of 14pt</p>
<h3> This is blue
<a href="C1_3.html"> colored </a> line</h3>
</Body>
</HTML>
```

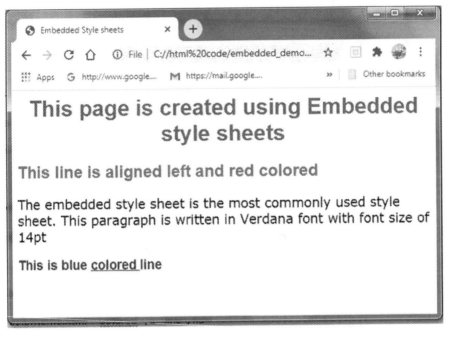

Figure 1-6. *Output of the embedded style settings*

External Style Sheets

When we want to apply a particular style to more than one web page, we can use external style sheets. This type of style sheet is stored in one .css file, and we must mention the name of that file in our relevant web pages. When we do so, the styles defined in .css file are applied to these web pages. Listing 1-4 is a simple program in which external style sheets are used.

Listing 1-4. External Style Sheet Example

```
<HTML>
<head>
<TITLE> External Style sheets </TITLE>
<link rel="stylesheet" type="txt/css" href=ex1.css"/>
</head>
```

```
<Body>
<h1 class="special"> <center>
This page is created using External style sheets </center>
</h1>
<h2> This line is aligned left and red colored </h2>
<p> The embedded style sheet is the most commonly used style
sheet. This paragraph is written in Verdana font with font size
of 14pt</p>
<h3>This is blue
<a href="C1_4.html"> colored </a> line</h3>
</Body>
</HTML>
```

The external style sheet is referenced in the href attribute as a value linking to ex1.css. Create a file named ex1.css in the same folder:

```
h1 {font-family:arial;}
h2 {
font-family:times new roman;
color:red;
left:20px;
}
h3 {
font-family:arial;
color:blue
}
p {
font-size:14pt;
font-family:cambria;
}
special {color:green }
```

JavaScript Basics

JavaScript is a scripting language (a lightweight programming language) and an interpreted language (executing without preliminary compilation). It is usually embedded directly into HTML pages and is designed to add interactivity to them. Java and JS are different.

JS attributes include the following:

- JS gives HTML designers a programming tool.

- JS can put dynamic text into an HTML page.

- JS can react to events.

- JS can read and write HTML elements.

- JS can be used to validate data.

- JavaScript can be used to apply AI,ML and DL techniques in the browser.

- JavaScript can be used to create cookies (Store and retrieve information on the visitor's computer).

Including the JavaScript

The HTML `<script>` tag is used to insert a script (JS) into an HTML page:

```
<script type="text/javascript">
    document.write("Hello World!");
</script>
```

The `<script>` tag is used to embed a client-side script. The `<script>` element either contains scripting statements or points to an external script file through the `src` attribute.

Where to Insert JS Scripts

You can include scripts in the head, body, or external JavaScript file (.js). Scripts in the head section (Listing 1-5) will be executed when the head section is invoked. Figure 1-7 shows the corresponding output. Scripts in the body section executes while the page loads (Listing 1-6), and Figure 1-8 shows the corresponding output.

Listing 1-5. JavaScript Inside the Head Section

```html
<html>
<head>
<script type="text/javascript">
function msg(){
 alert("Hello message");
}
</script>
</head>
<body>
<p>Welcome to JavaScript</p>
<form>
<input type="button" value="click" onclick="msg()"/>
</form></body></html>
```

Figure 1-7. *JavaScript inside the head section*

Listing 1-6. JavaScript Inside the Body Section

```html
<html>
<body>
<p id="demo">Hello Java Script</p>
<script>
document.getElementById("demo").innerHTML = "Java Script within
the body!";
</script>
</body>
</html>
```

Figure 1-8. *JavaScript inside the body section*

Listing 1-7 provides the JS function external to the program, and
Listing 1-8 shows the HTML for the corresponding output in Figure 1-9.

Listing 1-7. Message.js

```
function msg(){
 alert("Hello I am Outside your program");
}
```

Listing 1-8. HTML for Click Button

```
<html>
<head>
<script type="text/javascript" src="message.js"></script>
</head>
```

21

```
<body>
<p>Program call to external JavaScript</p>
<form>
<input type="button" value="click" onclick="msg()"/>
</form>
</body>
</html>
```

Figure 1-9. *JS external to the program*

JavaScript for an Event-Driven Process

Dynamic website development is possible by leveraging event-driven programming with JS. Commonly, after a website page has stacked, the JS program keeps running (and waiting for an event to occur). If you interact with the web page, a JS script executes the code that corresponds with that interaction (event), and the behavior of the page changes based on the event. Figure 1-10 shows a typical event-driven process with the help of JS features.

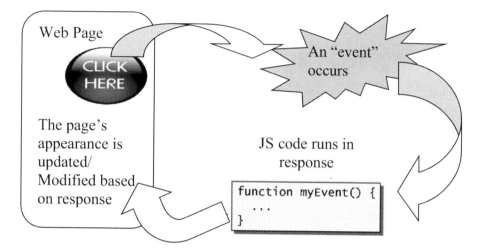

Figure 1-10. *Event-driven process on the web page with the help of JS code*

Document Object Model Manipulation

At the point when a web page is stacked, the browser (program) creates a Document Object Model (DOM) of the page. The HTML DOM is developed as a *tree of objects*. Through DOM, the elements (components) of the HTML can be manipulated, move across the web page and process efficiently.

The HTML DOM is an object model for HTML:

- HTML components as items(elements)

- Properties(attributes) for all HTML components

- Techniques for all HTML components

- Events for all HTML components

The HTML DOM is an application programming interface (API) for JavaScript:

- JS can include/change/delete HTML components.

- JS can include/change/delete HTML traits.

- JS can include/change/delete CSS styles.

- JS can respond to HTML events.

- JS can include/change/delete HTML events.

When creating site pages and applications, one of the main things you must do is control the archive structure. Developers typically do so by using the DOM, incorporating a lot of APIs to control HTML, and styling data that uses the document object.

Discovering HTML Elements: When you need to get to HTML components with JS, you need to discover the components first. You can do so in a few different ways:

- Discover HTML elements by ID

- Discover HTML elements by label name

- Discovering HTML elements by class name

- Discover HTML elements by CSS selectors

- Discover HTML elements by HTML object assortments

A web page while used in JS is a document, and JS provides an object called document, which is considered a complete web page. The document object offers various properties and methods to identify, access, and modify the web components/elements when loaded on the browser. To identify and access the DOM elements, JS uses the previously described discovery capability.

The following HTML source code shows such discovery at work:

```
<!DOCTYPE html>
<html>
<body>
<h2>Finding HTML Elements by Id</h2>
<p id="intro">Hello World!</p>
<p>This example demonstrates the <b>getElementsById</b>
method.</p>
<p id="demo1"></p>
<p id="demo2"></p>
<p class="intro">The DOM is very useful.</p>
<p class="intro">This example demonstrates the
<b>getElementsByClassName</b> method.</p>
<script>
var myElement = document.getElementById("intro");
document.getElementById("demo1").innerHTML =
"The text from the intro paragraph is " + myElement.innerHTML;
var x = document.getElementsByTagName("p");
document.getElementById("demo2").innerHTML =
'The text in first paragraph (index 0) is: ' + x[0].innerHTML;
var x1 = document.getElementsByClassName("intro");
document.getElementById("demo").innerHTML =
'The first paragraph (index 0) with class="intro": ' + x1[0].
innerHTML;
</script>
</body>
</html>
```

Introduction to jQuery

jQuery is a lightweight JS library that enables developers to compose less but accomplish more. The jQuery library enables the web programmers to do the following tasks easily:

- HTML and DOM element manipulation

- CSS management and control

- Provides event-driven techniques to trigger and react to an event on a web page such as mouse click, button click, key press, and so on

- Improves the functionality of Asynchronous JavaScript and XML (AJAX) calls for the exchange of information between two entities (such as client and server)

There are two ways to use the jQuery library in your program:

1. Download the jQuery library
   (https://code.jquery.com/jquery-3.5.1.min.js)
   from jQuery.com and store it in the same folder as that
   of the source code (HTML and CSS code) location and
   use it as follows:

   ```
   <head>
   <script src="jquery-3.5.1.min.js"></script>
   </head>
   ```

Or

2. If you are connected to the Internet, use the
    following link from Google CDN to include jQuery
    features:

```
<head>
<script src="https://ajax.googleapis.com/ajax/libs/
jquery/3.5.1/jquery.min.js">
</script>
</head>
```

Listing 1-9 shows how to use the jQuery library and its functionality,
and Figures 1-11 and 1-12 show its corresponding output.

Listing 1-9. Using the jQuery Library

```
<!DOCTYPE html>
<html>
<head>
<script src="jquery-3.5.1.min.js"></script>
<script>
$(document).ready(function(){
  $("button").click(function(){
    $("p").hide();
  });
});
</script>
</head>
<body>
<h2>jQuery Example</h2>
<p>first paragraph</p>
```

```
<p>second paragraph</p>
<button>hide</button>
</body>
</html>
```

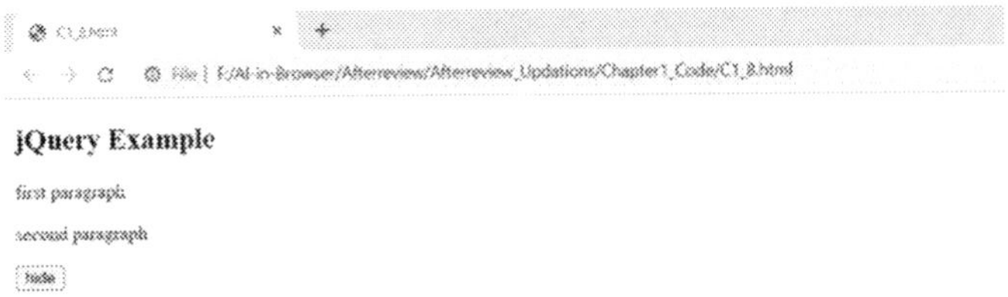

Figure 1-11. *Listing 1-9 output before the Hide button is clicked*

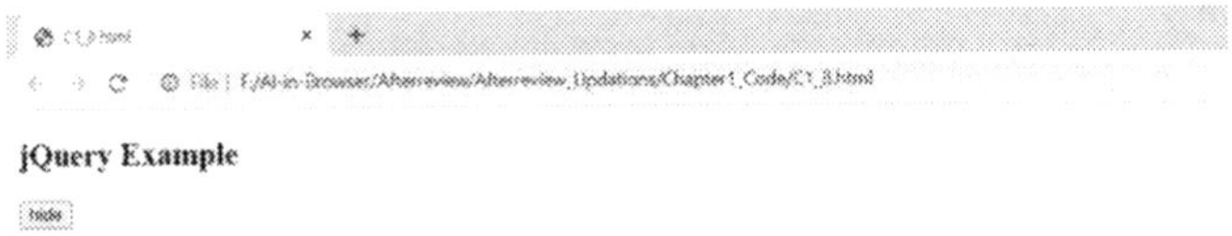

Figure 1-12. *Listing 1-9 output after the Hide button is clicked*

Summary

This chapter introduced ML and provided a practical overview of web design and development. Following are some key takeaways:

- HTML is the language that we use to structure the various pieces of our content and define their importance.

- CSS is the language that we use to style and design our web content to make it more lively.

- JS is the scripting language that we use to add dynamic usefulness to website pages.

- DOM describes the logical structure of documents (web pages) and the way a document is accessed and manipulated using the components (elements of the web pages).

- jQuery is a small JavaScript library that simplifies HTML document (web page) traversal and manipulation event handling, and animation.

You should now be able to start designing and developing applications that incorporate AI/ML in their web components.

References

Mitchell, Tom M. *Machine Learning*. McGraw-Hill, 1997.

Singh, Himanshu. *Practical Machine Learning and Image Processing*. Apress, 2019.

Marsland, Stephen. *Machine Learning: An Algorithmic Perspective*. Chapman & Hall/CRC Machine Learning & Pattern Recognition; 1st Edition, 2009.

bin Uzayr, Sufyan, Nicholas Cloud, and Tim Ambler. *JavaScript Frameworks for Modern Web Development: The Essential Frameworks, Libraries, and Tools to Learn Right Now*. Apress, 2019.

Cook, Craig, and David Schultz. *Beginning HTML with CSS and XHTML, Modern Guide and Reference.* Apress, 2007.

https://code.visualstudio.com/

https://netbeans.org/

https://www.jetbrains.com/pycharm/

Ferguson, Russ. *Beginning JavaScript, The Ultimate Guide to Modern JavaScript Development.* Apress, 2019.

CHAPTER 2

Browser-Based Data Processing

Now that you understand the basics of web development, this chapter introduces two JavaScript (JS) libraries: p5.js and ml5.js. The chapter also delves deeper into JS features and syntax related to various problem-solving and application-development implementations. It then discusses various ways to use graphics and machine learning (ML) application processing interface methods to actualize artificial intelligence (AI) in the browser.

Browser computer vision techniques, such as image classification, are also discussed relative to JS programming. In this chapter, you also work through practical examples of running web applications using the Node.js and Python Hypertext Transfer Protocol (HTTP) server programs.

JavaScript Libraries and API for ML on the Web

AI and ML are at the forefront of modern computing and are currently hot topics. How "smart" your computational frameworks are can factor into the success or failure (or optimization) of your applications' data processing.

ML is better via soft computing interfaces rather than via hard-wired ones. Although AI/ML is becoming ubiquitous, most web developers have

© Nagender Kumar Suryadevara 2021
N. K. Suryadevara, *Beginning Machine Learning in the Browser*,
https://doi.org/10.1007/978-1-4842-6843-8_2

yet to master it. However, ML is an inevitable advance in the development of human-machine interaction. The only issue I have with regard to this relates to certain software vendors. Anybody can begin developing applications on the web (this unrivaled, genuinely open, and dispersed stage), and at present open-source technologies support, to a large extent, the design and development of web applications. However, the key thing that matters now is the ability to apply the smart concepts onto ML interfaces.

Presently, ML on the web looks significantly more open and less standard focused than I would like. To train models or try and get bits of data from models, you must use the API library.

W3C WebML CG (Community Group)

The W3C calls for making and incorporating APIs optimized for ML into the web development arena that will eventually allow developers to create interoperable ML content on various platforms. Intel and Microsoft began this work, and I am pleased that some APIs have been developed, but now we need to utilize the features effectively to make ML on the web a reality and thus achieve the following:

- *Improved execution*: Results from the prepared model return quickly, with no system slowdown.

- *Disconnected (offline) usefulness*: Queries running on devices/gadgets do not rely on an association with a cloud computing administration (and so avoid the issues of latency, throughput, and connectedness inherent in cloud computing).

- *Upgraded protection (privacy)*: Incredibly, many cloud administrations offer already prepared models to run our solicitations. We need not send our privacy information to others.

Although incorporating browser intelligence promises exciting functionality, it is important to remember that certain restrictions (limitations) also apply, including the following:

- *Record size*: Previously prepared models will, in general, be extremely large (e.g., often several megabytes). Such large record sizes on the client side will result in I/O delays and be subject to RAM constraints.

- *Restricted performance*: Earlier browser programs are limited to single-thread JavaScript execution instances, with no provisions to utilize the core computing features of the device/gadget.

Presently, you can use JS libraries to converse with existing AI/ML models, or you can develop your intelligent program to run on a browser or electronic device/gadget. With a scientific learning model that leverages JS library software, with some forethought, and with a couple lines of code, you can now develop applications that induce intelligence in the browser.

Manipulating HTML Elements Using JS Libraries

The following subsections show how to use the two most popular JS libraries (p5.js and ml5.js) to implement various functions such as graphics and ML on the browser.

The ml5.js library makes ML approachable for a broad audience, including artists, creative coders, and students. The library provides access to ML algorithms and models in the browser. The p5.js library is for handling graphical processing unit (GPU)-accelerated mathematical operations and memory management for ML algorithms.

p5.js

The p5.js library is a JavaScript library for creative coding intended to make comprehensive coding available for designers, developers, teachers, students, and more. It is free and open-source programming; the tools to learn p5.js are available to everybody. The p5.js library incorporates Processing principles for the modern web. A p5.js library can be any JS code that extends or adds to existing JS code.

A p5.js library is classified as either a core library or a contributed library. As with programmer JS code, p5.js has a full toolbox of drawing utilities that support HTML5 objects for text, input, video, webcam, and sound. To include a p5.js library in the program, link it to your HTML file. The following code snippet shows what an HTML file linked with a p5.js library looks like:

```
<!doctype html>
<html>
<head>
<script src="p5.js"></script>
<script src="user_code.js"></script>
</head>
<body>
</body>
</html>
```

Note   You can download the p5.js (single file, full uncompressed version) or p5.min.js (single file, compressed version) library from this link. You want to ensure that the p5.js/p5.min.js library and the HTML file are in the same folder (computer system path).

To develop and execute programs with p5.js library functionality, you need an editor (Notepad++) and a web browser (Chrome or Firefox).

Drawing Graphical Objects

Listings 2-1a and 2-1b show the inclusion of the p5.js library with the user code p5ex1_index.html. Figure 2-1 shows the corresponding output.

Listing 2-1a. p5ex1_index.html

```
<!DOCTYPE html>
<html>
  <head>
    <meta charset="UTF-8">
    <title>Example#1 p5.js </title>

    <script type="text/javascript" src="p5.min.js"></script>
    <script type="text/javascript" src="p5ex1_user_code1.js">
    </script>
  </head>
  <body>
    <h1> Example #1: p5.js and user_code1.js </h1>
    <p>Program for linking p5.js library and user_code.js </p>
  </body>
</html>
```

Listing 2-1b. p5ex1_user_code1.js

```
function setup() {
  createCanvas(720, 400);
  background(200);
}
function draw() {
  rect(40, 120, 120, 40); // A rectangle
  ellipse(240, 240, 80, 80);   // An ellipse
  triangle(300, 100, 320, 100, 310, 80); //A triangle
}
```

35

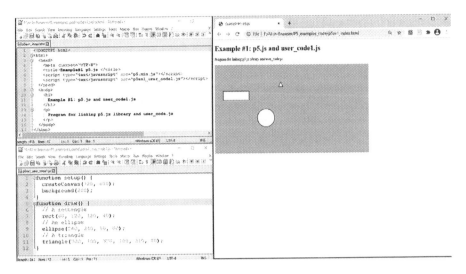

Figure 2-1. *Inclusion of p5.min.js library with the user JS code*

Manipulating DOM Objects

Listings 2-2a and 2-2b show how to create DOM objects using JS libraries (in this case, p5.js): p5ex2_index.html. Figure 2-2 shows the corresponding output.

Listing 2-2a. p5ex2_index.html

```
<!DOCTYPE html>
<html>
  <head>
    <meta charset="UTF-8">
    <title>Example#2 p5.js </title>
    <script type="text/javascript" src="p5.min.js"></script>
    <script type="text/javascript" src="p5ex2_user_code2.js">
    </script>
  </head>
```

```
<body>
   <h1> Example #2: p5.js and user_code2.js </h1>
   <p>Program for manipulating DOM objects using p5.js library </p>
</body>
</html>
```

Listing 2-2b. p5ex2_user_code2.js

```
var mycanvas,myh1;
function setup() {
  mycanvas = createCanvas(150, 150);
  mycanvas.position(200, 250);
  myh1 = createElement('h1', 'h1-New DOM Object .');
  myh1.position(100, 150);
  createP("****This is a new Paragraph*****");
}
function draw() {
  background(150, 150);
  fill(255, 0, 0);
 }
```

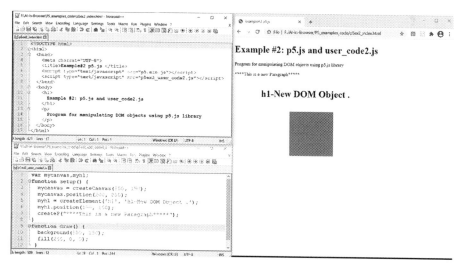

Figure 2-2. *Creating DOM objects using JS libraries (in this case, p5.js)*

DOM onEvent(mousePressed) Handling

Listings 2-3a and 2-3b provide the programs for calling DOM objects based on events using the p5.js library. Figure 2-3 shows the corresponding output.

Listing 2-3a. p5ex3_index.html

```
<!DOCTYPE html>
<html>
  <head>
    <meta charset="UTF-8">
    <title>Example#3 p5.js </title>
    <script type="text/javascript" src="p5.min.js"></script>
    <script type="text/javascript" src="p5ex3_user_code3.js">
    </script>
  </head>
  <body>
    <h1>Example #3: p5.js and user_code3.js </h1>
    <p>Program for calling DOM objects based on events using
    p5.js   library </p>
  </body>
</html>
```

Listing 2-3b. p5ex3_user_code3.js

```
var bgcolor,button;
function setup() {
  canvas = createCanvas(200, 200);
  bgcolor = color(200);
  button = createButton('Click this Button to change the color');
  button.position(250,150);
  button.mousePressed(changeColor);
}
```

```
function changeColor() {
  bgcolor = color(random(255));
}
function draw() {
  background(bgcolor);
 }
```

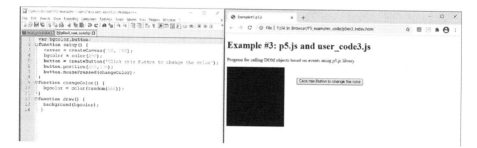

Figure 2-3. *Using the p5.js library to call DOM objects based on events*

Multiple DOM Objects onEvent Handling

Listings 2-4a and 2-4b show interaction of various HTML elements using the p5.js library. Figure 2-4 shows the corresponding output.

Listing 2-4a. p5ex4_index.html

```
<!DOCTYPE html>
<html>
  <head>
    <meta charset="UTF-8">
    <title>Example#4 p5.js </title>
    <script type="text/javascript" src="p5.min.js"></script>
    <script type="text/javascript" src="p5ex4_user_code4.js">
    </script>
  </head>
```

```
<body>
  <h1> Example #4: p5.js and user_code4.js </h1>
  <p> Program for interacting various HTML elements using
  p5.js library
  </p>
</body>
</html>
```

Listing 2-4b. p5ex4_user_code4.js

```
var mybgcolor,mybutton,myslider1,myinput1,myname;
function setup() {
  mycanvas = createCanvas(200, 200);
  mybgcolor = color(200);
  myname = createP('Your name!');
  mybutton = createButton('Click to resize the circle');
  mybutton.mousePressed(changeColor);
  myslider1 = createSlider(10, 100, 86);
  myinput1 = createInput('Enter your name::');
}
function changeColor() {
  mybgcolor = color(random(255));
}

function draw() {
  background(mybgcolor);
  fill(255, 0, 175);
  ellipse(100, 100, myslider1.value(), myslider1.value());
  myname.html(myinput1.value());
  text(myinput1.value(), 10, 20);
}
```

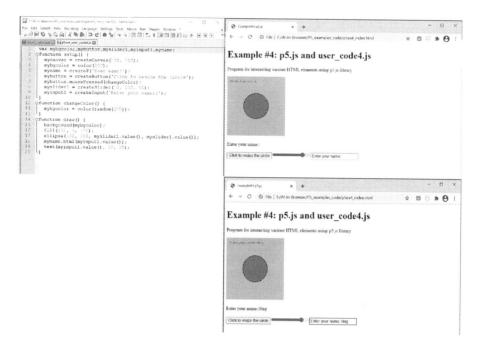

Figure 2-4. *Using the p5.js library to create interactivity between various HTML elements*

HTML Interactive Elements

Listings 2-5a and 2-5b show another example for interacting with various HTML elements using the p5.js library. Figure 2-5 shows the corresponding output.

Listing 2-5a. p5ex5_index.html

```html
<!DOCTYPE html>
<html>
  <head>
    <meta charset="UTF-8">
    <title>Example#5 p5.js </title>
    <script type="text/javascript" src="p5.min.js"></script>
```

41

```
    <script type="text/javascript" src="p5ex5_user_code5.js">
    </script>
  </head>
  <body>
    <h1>Example #5: p5.js and user_code5.js</h1>
    <p> Program for interacting various HTML elements using
    p5.js library
    </p>
  </body>
</html>
```

Listing 2-5b. p5ex5_user_code5.js

```
var bgcolor1,mybutton1,myslider1,mynameInput,mynamepar;
function setup() {
  mycanvas = createCanvas(200, 200);
  mycanvas.mouseOver(overpara);
  mycanvas.mouseOut(outpara);
  mycanvas.mousePressed(changeColor);
  bgcolor1 = color(200);
  mynamepar = createP('Dummy Text!');
  mybutton1 = createButton('Click');
  mybutton1.mousePressed(changeColor);
  myslider1 = createSlider(10, 100, 86);
  mynameInput = createInput('Enter your name::');
  mynamepar.mouseOver(overpara);
  mynamepar.mouseOut(outpara);
  mynameInput.changed(updateText);
  }
function updateText(){mynamepar.html(mynameInput.value()); }
function overpara()  {mynamepar.html('your mouse is over me');}
function outpara()   {mynamepar.html('your mouse is out');}
```

```
function changeColor(){bgcolor1 = color(random(255));}
function draw(){ background(bgcolor1);
            fill(255, 0, 175);
            ellipse(100, 100, myslider1.value(), myslider1.
            value());
                text(mynameInput.value(), 10, 20);
            }
```

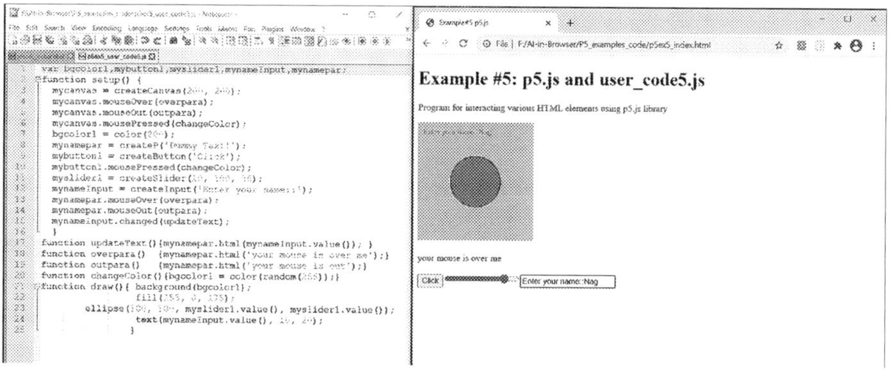

Figure 2-5. *Using the p5.js library to create HTML interactive elements*

Interaction with HTML and CSS Elements

Listings 2-6a and 2-6b show the interaction of various HTML elements using the p5.js library with CSS elements. Figure 2-6 shows the corresponding output.

Listing 2-6a. p5ex6_index.html

```
<!DOCTYPE html>
<html>
  <head>
    <meta charset="UTF-8">
    <title>Example #6 p5.js and CSS </title>
```

```
    <script type="text/javascript" src="p5.min.js"></script>
    <style>
      #item1 {
        font-size: 52pt;
      }
      .paraclass {
        font-size: 26pt;
        background-color: #EOF;
      }
      p {  padding: 10pt;  }
    </style>
  </head>

<body>
<h1>Example #6: p5.js for CSS selectors and user_code6.js</h1>
<p>Program for interacting with CSSelements using p5.js
library</p>
<p id = "item1" class="paraclass">Items</p>
<p class="paraclass">Paragraph2</p>
<p class="paraclass">Paragraph3</p>
<p>Paragraph4.</p>
</body>
</html>
```

Listing 2-6b. p5ex6_user_code6.js

```
function setup() {}
function draw() {}
```

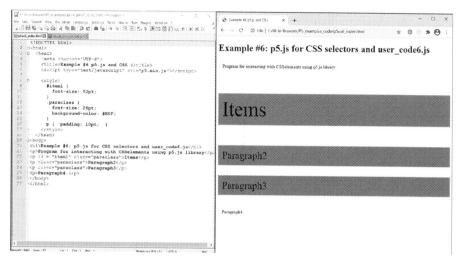

Figure 2-6. *p5.js with CSS elements example*

Hierarchical (Parent-Child) Interaction of DOM Elements

Listings 2-7a and 2-7b show p5.js with parent-child DOM elements. Figure 2-7 shows the corresponding output.

Listing 2-7a. p5ex7_index.html

```
<!DOCTYPE html>
<html>
<head>
<meta charset="UTF-8">
<title>Multi level (Parent-Child)DOM elements </title>
<script type="text/javascript" src="p5.min.js"></script>
<script type="text/javascript" src="p5ex7_user_code7.js">
</script>
<style> body{padding:0;margin:0;}canvas{vertical-align:top;}
</style>
</head>
```

45

```
<body>
<h1>Example #7::Parent and Child DOM Elements</h1>
<p id="canvaspara">This paragraph should include the canvas.</p>
 <p> I am a parent and a child. </p>
 <h1>List of Emotions</h1>
    <button id="button">Click for the Emotion</button>
    <ol id="listofemotions">  </ol>
</body>
</html>
```

Listing 2-7b. p5ex7_user_code7.js

```javascript
var emotions = ['happy', 'sad', 'neutral', 'angry'];
function setup() {
   var canvas1 = createCanvas(300, 300);
   canvas1.parent("canvaspara");
  var button1 = select('#button');
  button1.mousePressed(addItem1);
}
function addItem1() {
  var r = floor(random(0, emotions.length));
  var li = createElement('li', emotions[r]);
  li.parent('listofemotions');
}
function draw(){
     background(150);
}
```

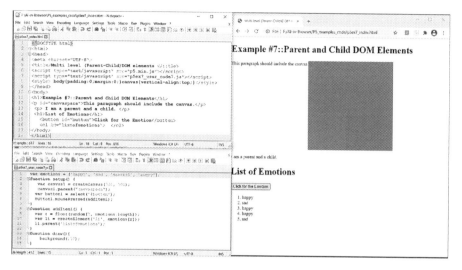

Figure 2-7. *Using p5.js with parent-child DOM elements*

Accessing DOM Parent-Child Elements Using Variables

Listings 2-8a and 2-8b show parent-child elements with variables using p5.js. Figure 2-8 shows the corresponding output.

Listing 2-8a. p5ex8_index.html

```
<!DOCTYPE html>
<html>
  <head>
    <meta charset="UTF-8">
    <title> Example #8 parent()_and_child() with variables
    </title>
    <script type="text/javascript" src="p5.min.js"></script>
    <script type="text/javascript" src="p5ex8_user_code8.js">
    </script>
```

47

```
  <style> body {padding: 0; margin: 0;} canvas {vertical-
  align: top;}
  </style>
  </head>
  <body>
  </body>
</html>
```

Listing 2-8b. p5ex8_user_code8.js

```
var p;
function setup() {
  noCanvas();
  p = createP('This is a link to click for: ');
  p.style('background-color','#AAA');
  p.style('padding', '48px');
  var a = createA('#', 'flower');
  a.mousePressed(addpic);
  a.parent(p);
}
function addpic() {
  var img = createImg('flower1.jpg');
  img.size(100, 100);
  img.parent(p);
  }
```

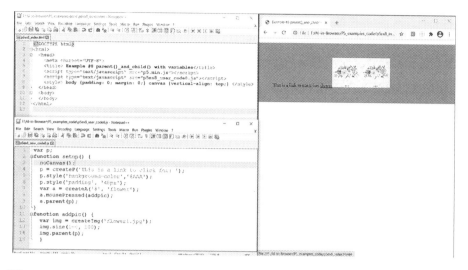

Figure 2-8. *p5.js with parent-child variables example*

Graphics and Interactive Processing in the Browser Using p5.js

This section provides examples that show how to use p5.js libraries to implement a browser's interactive and graphics features. Listings 2-9a and 2-9b show how to use the p5.js library to implement graphics functions to illustrate mouse press events. Figure 2-9 shows the corresponding output.

Listing 2-9a. p5_graphics_ex_index.html

```
<!DOCTYPE html>
<html>
<head>
  <script src="p5.min.js"></script>
  <meta charset="utf-8" />
</head>
```

```html
<body>
<script src="p5_graphics_ex1_user_code1.js"></script>
</body>
</html>
```

Listing 2-9b. p5_graphics_ex1_user_code1.js

```javascript
let x = 100;
let y = 100;
let extraCanvas1;
function setup()
{
  createCanvas(300, 300);
  extraCanvas1 = createGraphics(300, 300);
  extraCanvas1.clear();
 }

function draw()
{
  background(255,204,0);
  x += random(-5, 5);
  y += random(-5, 5);
  if (mouseIsPressed) {
    extraCanvas1.fill(255, 150);
    extraCanvas1.noStroke();
    extraCanvas1.ellipse(mouseX, mouseY, 60, 60);
  }
  image(extraCanvas1, 0, 0);
  fill('blue');   stroke(255);
  rectMode(CENTER);   rect(x, y, 20, 20);
}
```

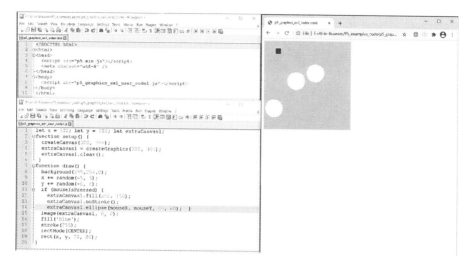

Figure 2-9. *Graphics functions with mouse press event using p5.js library*

Interactive Graphics Application

Listings 2-10a and 2-10b show a graphics script for a bouncing ball illustration using the p5.js library. Figure 2-10 shows the corresponding output.

Listing 2-10a. p5_graphics_ex2_index.html

```
<!DOCTYPE html>
<html>
<head>
  <script src="p5.min.js"></script>
  <meta charset="utf-8" />
</head>
<body>
<script src="p5_graphics_ex2_user_code2.js"></script>
</body>
</html>
```

Listing 2-10b. p5_graphics_ex2_user_code2.js

```
var ball = {
  x: 300,
  y: 200,
  xspeed: 4,
  yspeed: -3
};
function setup() {
  createCanvas(600, 400);
}
function draw() {
  background('blue');
  move();
  bounce();
  display();
}
function bounce() {
  if (ball.x > width || ball.x < 0) {
    ball.xspeed = ball.xspeed * -1;
  }
  if (ball.y > height || ball.y < 0) {
    ball.yspeed = ball.yspeed * -1;
  }
}
function display() {
  stroke(255);
  strokeWeight(4);
  fill(200, 0, 200);
  ellipse(ball.x, ball.y, 36, 36);
}
```

```
function move() {
  ball.x = ball.x + ball.xspeed;
  ball.y = ball.y + ball.yspeed;
}
```

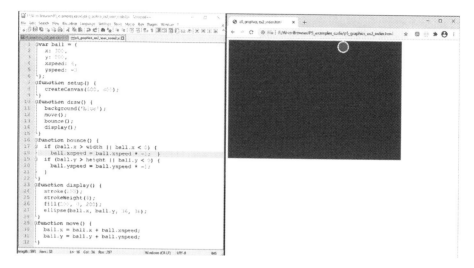

Figure 2-10. *p5.js graphics script for bouncing ball*

Object Instance, Storage of Multiple Values, and Loop Through Object

Listings 2-11a and 2-11b show a p5.js graphics function using class, object, array, and loop features. Figure 2-11 shows the corresponding output.

Listing 2-11a. p5_graphics_ex3_index.html

```
<!DOCTYPE html>
<html>
<head>
  <script src="p5.min.js"></script>
  <meta charset="utf-8" />
</head>
```

```
<body>
<script src="p5_graphics_ex3_user_code3.js"></script>
</body>
</html>
```

Listing 2-11b. p5_graphics_ex3_user_code3.js

```
var circles = [100, 25, 46, 72];
let square1;
let square2;
function setup() {
  createCanvas(500, 400);
  square1 = new Square();
  square2 = new Square();
}

function draw() {
  background('red');
  for (var i = 0; i < 4; i++) {
    stroke(255);
    fill(51);
    ellipse(i * 100 + 100, 200, circles[i], circles[i]);
  }
  square1.move();
  square1.show();
  square2.move();
  square2.show();
}
class Square {
  constructor(x, y, r) {
    this.x = 200;
```

```
    this.y = 150;
  }
move() {
    this.x = this.x + random(-5, 5);
    this.y = this.y + random(-5, 5);
  }
  show() {
    stroke(255);
    strokeWeight(4);
    noFill();
    square(this.x, this.y, 36, 6);
  }
}
```

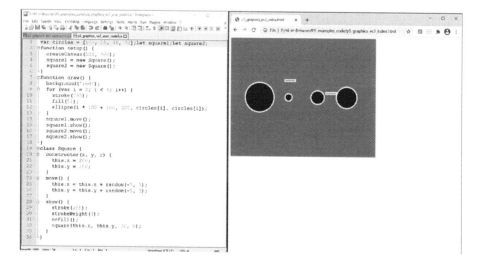

Figure 2-11. *p5.js graphics function that uses class, object, array, and loop features*

Getting Started with Machine Learning in the Browser Using ml5.js and p5.js

The ml5.js library makes AI accessible to creative coders. The library was created at New York University, and it was openly released in July 2018. The library gives access to AI methods and models in the program, expanding on TensorFlow.js and with no other outside dependencies. The ml5.js library makes life simpler for those who are new to the ML field. You can find more information at this link.

To develop and execute programs that incorporate p5.js and ml5.js libraries, you need the following:

> Editor: Visual Studio Code or Notepad++
>
> Web browser: Chrome or Firefox
>
> Sample images and datasets for developing ML applications

Design, Develop, and Execute Programs Locally

There are two methods for running a local web server on your computer to develop and execute your programs on the local computer.

Method 1: Using Python – HTTP Server

1. Install Python 3+ on your computer.

2. `cd /path_to/ml5_p5-examples` (At the command prompt, go to the folder that holds your ml5/p5 programs.)

3. python -m http.server 8081

4. In the browser URL, type the following:
   localhost:8081/indexfilename

Listings 2-12a and 2-12b show the ml5.js library using a Python web server for image classification. Figure 2-12 shows the corresponding output.

Listing 2-12a. ml5_ex1_index.html

```html
<html>
<head>
  <meta charset="UTF-8">
  <title>Image Classification Example</title>
  <script src="ml5.min.js" type="text/javascript"></script>
</head>
<body>
  <h1>Image classification using MobileNet model</h1>
  <p>The MobileNet model labeled this as
    <span id="result">... </span> with a confidence of
    <span id="probability">...</span>.
  </p>
  <img src="images/bird1.png" id="image" width="400" />
  <script src="ml5_ex1_user_code1.js"></script>
</body>
</html>
```

Listing 2-12b. ml5_ex1_user_code1.js

```javascript
const image = document.getElementById('image');
const result = document.getElementById('result');
const probability = document.getElementById('probability');
ml5.imageClassifier('MobileNet')
```

```
  .then(classifier => classifier.classify(image))
  .then(results => {
    result.innerText = results[0].label;
    probability.innerText = results[0].confidence.toFixed(4);
  });
```

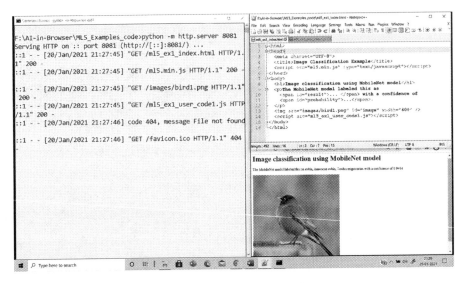

Figure 2-12. *Usage of ml5.js library along with Python server and Notepad++ (example related to image classification)*

Method 2: Using Visual Studio Code Editor with Node.js Live Server

1. Download and install Node.js from this link.

2. Install Node Package Manager (NPM) from this link.

3. Download and install Visual Studio Code from this link.

4. Open the Visual Studio Code editor and click the GoLive button so that the output of the program can be seen in the browser.

The following examples show the execution of the programs under this method.

Listing 2-13 is an example of an image classification using Node.js server. The outputs related to different images are shown in Figure 2-13(a), Figure 2-13(b), Figure 2-13(c), and Figure 2-13(d).

Listing 2-13. Image Classification Using the Node.js Server

```
<html>
<head>
  <meta charset="UTF-8">
  <title>Image Classification Example</title>
  <script src="ml5.min.js" type="text/javascript"></script>
</head>
<body>
  <h1>Image classification using MobileNet model</h1>
  <p>The MobileNet model labeled this as
    <span id="result">... </span> with a confidence of
    <span id="probability">...</span>.
  </p>
  <img src="images/bird1.png" id="image" width="400" />
  <script src="ml5_ex1_user_code1.js"></script>
</body>
</html>
ml5_ex1_1_user_code1.js
const image = document.getElementById('image');
const result = document.getElementById('result');
const probability = document.getElementById('probability');
ml5.imageClassifier('MobileNet')
  .then(classifier => classifier.classify(image))
```

```
.then(results => {
  result.innerText = results[0].label;
  probability.innerText = results[0].confidence.toFixed(4);
});
```

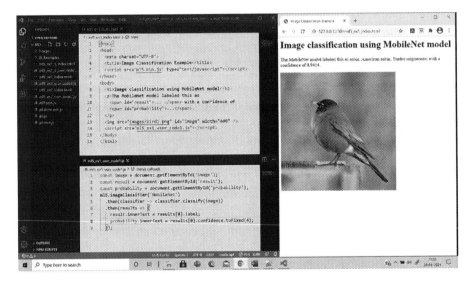

Figure 2-13(a). *Image classification(Example:Bird)using the Node.js server and Visual Studio Code*

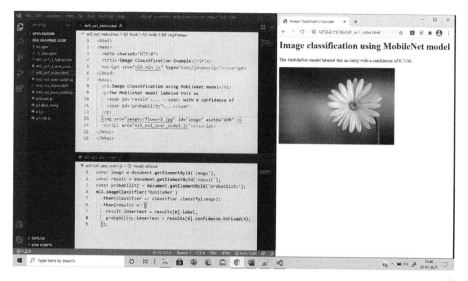

Figure 2-13(b). *Image Classification(Example:Flower) using the Node.js server and Visual Studio Code*

The ml5.js library's methods and functions are asynchronous (because ML models can take significant amounts of time to process input and generate output).

Using Promises   The ml5.js library also supports promises. If no callback is provided to any asynchronous function, a promise is returned. With promises, the image classification example can be used in the following way.

61

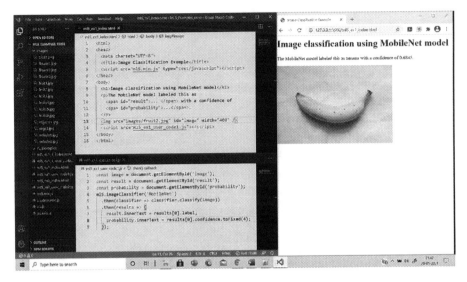

Figure 2-13(c). *Image classification (Example:Fruit) using the Node.js server and Visual Studion Code*

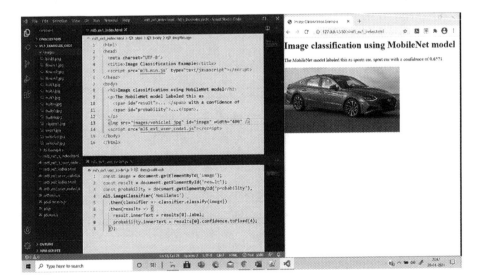

Figure 2-13(d). *Image classification (Example:Vehicle) using Node.js server and Visual Studio Code*

Note   In the preceding example, a MobileNet library is used for illustration. MobileNet is a convolutional neural network (CNN) architecture model for image classification and mobile vision. It is best suited for web browsers because browsers have limitations related to computation, graphic processing, and storage.

Summary

AI/ML researchers have provided us a huge number of functionalities in the form of libraries, making the implementation of AI/ML as easy as including the various libraries in our solution space.

In this chapter, you learned how to use two JS libraries (p5.js and ml5.js) that enable you to build and deploy interactive graphics and ML applications on the browser. These new and improved libraries have proven themselves effective in numerous utilization cases.

By using these libraries, you can compose code for various real-time applications on the browser in a simpler and more naturally intuitive way.

References

https://p5js.org/

https://p5js.org/reference/

McCarthy, Lauren. *Getting Started with p5.js: Making Interactive Graphics in JavaScript and Processing.* Make Community, 2015.

https://ml5js.org/

https://blog.etereo.io/machine-learning-
in-the-browser-for-the-entire-family-
125ca5a449a1

https://towardsdatascience.com/introduction-
to-ml5-js-3fe51d6a4661

https://www.opensourceforu.com/2020/02/ml5-
js-machine-learning-made-more-user-friendly/

https://github.com/processing/p5.js?files=1

https://github.com/ml5js

CHAPTER 3

Human Pose Estimation in the Browser

This chapter describes human pose estimation, a computer vision advancement that seeks to understand human movement through pictures and videos. The chapter discusses the various ways to estimate human poses through machine learning (ML) methods, with a focus on Dan Oved's PoseNet method.

PoseNet is an ML model that allows for real-time human pose estimation by finding different points on the human body and face. This chapter shows you step by step how to write the code to recognize various poses (keypoints) of the human face. Programming instructions teach you how to collect and manage the data related to these keypoints. This procedure will help you estimate other vital human pose keypoints and understand their classification patterns, as discussed in the following chapters.

© Nagender Kumar Suryadevara 2021
N. K. Suryadevara, *Beginning Machine Learning in the Browser*,
https://doi.org/10.1007/978-1-4842-6843-8_3

Human Pose at a Glance

Human pose assessment is an important topic that the computer vision community has been grappling with for the past few decades. It is a pivotal advancement toward understanding individuals in pictures and videos.

Human pose estimation is done by defining joints of a human body (otherwise called *keypoints*: elbows, wrists, and so on) in still images or videos. It is also characterized as the quest for a specific pose in the space of all poses.

The fundamentals of a human 2D pose is the estimate of a 2D coordinate (x, y) for each joint of the human pose from an RGB (red, green, blue) image. Human 2D pose estimation can be used to assess (and analyze and hopefully improve) the specific movements of a football player (or other sportsperson) during a game. A gait analysis can be monitored for early diagnosis of potential problems related to such.

PoseNet vs. OpenPose

You can enable human pose estimation on computing devices by utilizing various libraries such as PoseNet developed by Ross Wightman and from Carnegie Mellon University. PoseNet is built to run on lightweight computing devices such as browsers and mobile phones, whereas OpenPose is much more precise and intended to be run on graphical processing unit (GPU)-powered systems.

Note   It is more expensive and complex (including less flexibility) to run AI/ML programs on GPU-powered systems as compared to on non-GPU electronic devices.

PoseNet output for a 2D system is processed fast, but it may miss a number poses throughout the video, which you can tell by the flickering and disappearing skeleton. Nevertheless, if you really need to use PoseNet on resource-constrained devices such as on a mobile phone or an embedded system with less computational resources (e.g., limited processing capability, less storage, and fewer communication workloads and fast response), PoseNet is the right choice. Human pose estimation using PoseNet will enable the user to make smart decisions in near real time when the AI methods are executed on the browser or the lightweight computational resources.

You can improve PoseNet estimation accuracy with better data processing procedures at the web application to generate better inferences.

Human Pose Estimation Using Neural Networks

In the literature, numerous human pose estimation methods use neural network philosophy proposed by various research groups. The following sections briefly describe the evolution of the human pose estimation methods.

DeepPose: Human Pose Estimation via Deep Neural Networks

DeepPose was the main significant paper that applied deep learning (DL) to human pose assessment. It accomplished state-of-the-art (SOTA) execution and beat existing models. In this methodology, pose assessment is detailed, like a convolutional neural network (CNN)-based relapse issue toward body joints. In addition, the method utilizes a course of regressors to refine the posture appraisals and to improve gauges. One significant thing this methodology does is explain posture in comprehensive design (i.e., whether certain joints are covered up; they can be assessed if the posture is contemplated comprehensively). The paper contends that CNNs typically give possible poses and show reliable results. The xy coordinate values generated from the method specified by the authors are not accurate as it shows the multifaceted (multiple set of values) that are inadequate to specific joints of human body.

Efficient Object Localization Using Convolutional Networks

This approach creates heatmaps by running a picture through various resolutions to capture the joints at an assortment of scales. The yield is a discrete heatmap rather than a nonstop relapse. A heatmap predicts the likelihood of the common happening at every pixel. This yield model is useful, and a number of the papers that followed anticipated heatmaps rather than direct regression. The authors have considered the joint utilization of a CNN and graphical model.

Convolutional Pose Machines

Convolutional pose machines are differentiable, and their multistage engineering can be prepared start to finish. They give a successive forecast system to learning-rich specific spatial models and work very well for human posture. One real inspirations of this paper is to learn long-range spatial connections, and they show this can be accomplished by utilizing deep multistage networks. The paper utilized moderate management after each phase to avoid the issue of evaporating inclinations, which is a typical issue for profound multistage organizations.

Human Pose Estimation with Iterative Error Feedback

This method directly foresees the outcomes in one go. The method utilize a self-adjusting model that logically changes an underlying arrangement by taking care of feedback data, and this cycle is called *iterative error feedback*.

Stacked Hourglass Networks for Human Pose Estimation

A stacked hourglass network is a novel and intuitive design that beats every past technique. It is called a stacked hourglass network because the organization comprises steps of pooling and upsampling layers (resembling an hourglass), and these are stacked together. The plan of the hourglass is driven by the need to catch data at each scale.

Simple Baselines for Human Pose Estimation and Tracking

Earlier methodologies work well overall but are unpredictable. Accomplished the best in class at mean average precision (mAP) of 73.7% on Common Objects in Contest (COCO) dataset. The organization structure is straightforward and comprises a residual neural network (ResNet) and a few deconvolutional layers toward the end.

Deep High-Resolution Representation Learning for Human Pose Estimation

The high-resoulution network model is better than the previous methods with respect to the single-person keypoint detection and multiperson pose estimation using the particular dataset. This method works well when compared to the previous mentioned methods.

This section briefly described the most outstanding and influential models in human pose estimation. The approaches were based on the DL methodology with varying percentages of accuracy.

Using the ml5.js:posenet() Method

Although various methods enable us to estimate human pose keypoints, Dan Oved's PoseNet model does the real-time human pose estimation on the browser and resource-constrained computing devices. This section outlines his steps for collecting human pose estimation using the ml5. posenet method.

Note   We will add the instructions (code) step by step in the 1.js script file to capture the video and identify the human pose keypoints so that you can better understand the development of the browser application.

Step 1A. Include ml5.js and p5.js libraries for the PoseNet model (Listing 3-1a).

Listing 3-1a. 1.html

```
<html>
<head>
<h1> <center> Demo#1</center></h1>
<h2> <center> Posenet using m15.posenet</center> </h2>
<h3> <center> The standard ML5.JS and P5.JS libraries are
included </center> </h3>
<script src="p5.js"</script>
<script src="m15.min.js"></script>
<meta charset="utf-8">
<link rel="stylesheet" type="text/css" href="style.css">
</head>
<body>
<script src="1.js"> </script>
</body>
</html>
```

Step 1B. See the 1.js script (Listing 3-1b) to capture the video. Main file (1.html) programming instructions remain the same.

Listing 3-1b. 1.js

```
Let video;
Function setup() {
      createCanvas(640,480);
      video=createCapture(VIDEO);
}
Function draw() {
      Image(video,0,0);
}
```

Figure 3-1 shows the corresponding output for the code. You must click the Allow button to view the face.

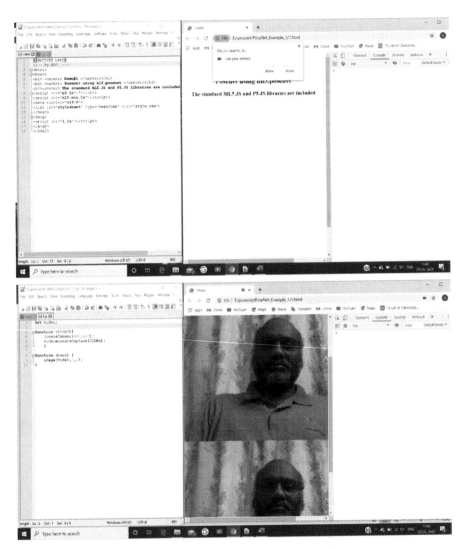

Figure 3-1. *Screenshot (output) related to the 1.html and 1.js script to capture the browser webcam video after clicking the Allow button. The two videos depict i) the original video capture and ii) the captured video drawn onto the canvas*

Step 2. Add the `video.hide()` function to hide the captured video and show only the canvas video in the 1.js script (Listing 3-2). Figure 3-2 shows the corresponding output.

Listing 3-2. Adding video.hide()

```
Let video;
Function setup() {
      createCanvas(640,480);
      video=createCapture(VIDEO);
      video.hide();
}
Function draw() {
      Image(video,0,0);
}
```

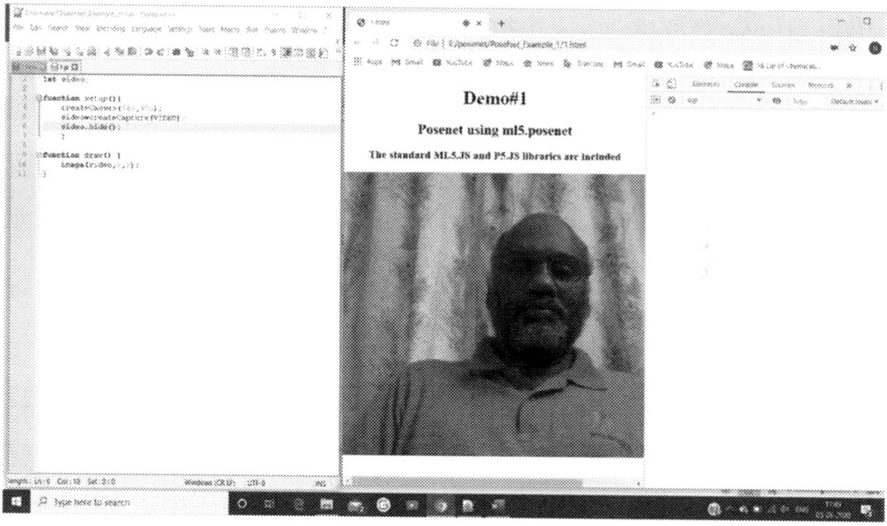

Figure 3-2. *Screenshot (output). Display only the captured video on the canvas; the original video is hidden*

73

Step 3. Invoke the m15.poseNet( ) method in the 1.js script (Listing 3-3). Figure 3-3 shows the output.

Listing 3-3. Invoking ml5.poseNet( )

```
Let video;
Let posenet;
Function setup() {
      createCanvas(640,480);
      video=createCapture(VIDEO);
video.hide();
posenet=m15.poseNet(video.modelready);
}
Function modelready() {
      Console.log('posenet model is ready');
}

Function draw() {
      Image(video,0,0);
}
```

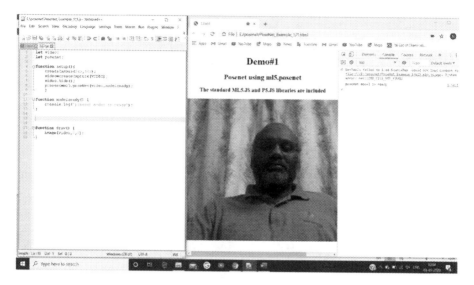

Figure 3-3. *Screenshot (output) on calling the method* m15.poseNet()*. The model is loaded onto the browser application, as shown on the browser console*

Step 4. Real-time poses are estimated for this poseNet.on( ) method in the 1.js, (i.e., listening to the new poses) (Listing 3-4). Figure 3-4 shows the corresponding output.

Listing 3-4. poseNet.on( )

```
Let video;
Let posenet;
Function setup() {
    createCanvas(640,480);
    video=createCapture(VIDEO);
    video.hide();
    posenet=m15.poseNet(video.modelready);
    posenet.on('pose',showPoses);
}
```

```
Function showPoses(poses) {
    console.log(poses)
}
Function modelready() {
    console.log('posenet model is ready');
}
Function draw() {
    Image(video,0,0);
}
```

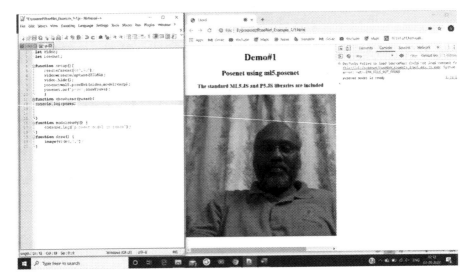

Figure 3-4. *Screenshot (output) once the PoseNet model is loaded and poseNet.on() listens to the new poses of the user*

Step 5. Add function showPoses() in the 1.js script file so that the data related to the poses is stored in the corresponding tensors, which are shown in the browser console (Listing 3-5). Figure 3-5 shows the corresponding output.

Listing 3-5. Adding showPoses()

```
Let video;
Let posenet;
Function setup() {
      createCanvas(640,480);
      video=createCapture(VIDEO);
      video.hide();
      posenet=m15.poseNet(video.modelready);
      posenet.on('pose',showPoses);
}
Function showPoses(poses) {
      console.log(poses)
}
Function modelready() {
      console.log('posenet model is ready');
}
Function draw() {
      Image(video,0,0);
}
```

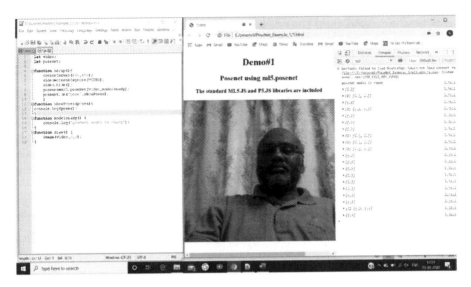

Figure 3-5. *Screenshot (output). Data as collected in the tensors is shown in the browser console*

Step 6. Add an array of poses collected in the object poses in 1.js script file (Listing 3-6). Figure 3-6 shows the corresponding output.

Listing 3-6. Array of Poses Collected in the Object Poses

```
Let video;
Let posenet;
Function setup() {
     createCanvas(640,480);
     video=createCapture(VIDEO);
     video.hide();
     posenet=m15.poseNet(video.modelready);
     posenet.on('pose',showPoses);
}
Function showPoses(poses) {
     console.log(poses)
}
```

```
Function modelready() {
      console.log('posenet model is ready');
}
Function draw() {
      Image(video,0,0);
}
```

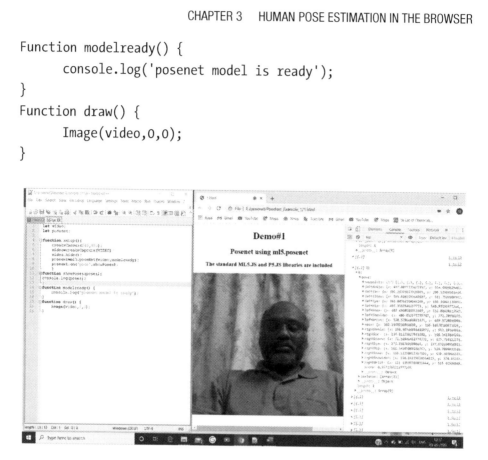

Figure 3-6. *Screenshot (output). An array of poses as collected in the object poses is shown in the browser console*

Step 7. poseNet.on () returns an array with a single object of several poses (keypoints), and recognizes the pose such as nose x and y coordinates by altering the function draw() in 1.js script file (Listing 3-7). Figure 3-7 shows the corresponding output.

Listing 3-7. Altering the draw() Function by Adding the ellipse Method to Display the Specific Keypoints

```
Let video;
Let posenet;
```

```
Let pose;
Function setup() {
      createCanvas(640,480);
      video=createCapture(VIDEO);
video.hide();
posenet=m15.poseNet(video.modelready);
posenet.on('pose',showPoses);
}

Function showPoses(numberofposes) {
console.log(numberofposes);
if(numberofposes.length>0)
{
      Pose=numberofposes[0].pose;
}
}

Function modelready() {
      console.log('posenet model is ready');
}

Function draw() {
      Image(video,0,0);
      If(pose) {
fill(255,0,0);
ellipse(pose.nose.x,pose.y,64);}
}
```

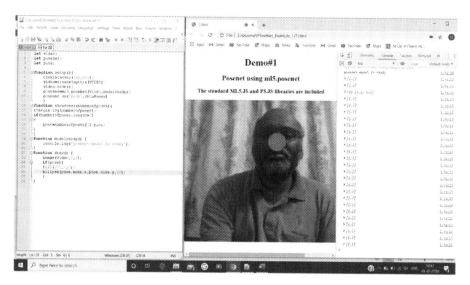

Figure 3-7. *Screenshot (output) showing a single object with several poses and recognizing the specific pose (keypoint): nose x and y coordinates with a red ellipse*

Step 8. Add instructions (code) in the 1.js script file draw() function to recognize two different human poses (keypoints): nose and ear (Listing 3-8). Figure 3-8 shows the corresponding output.

Listing 3-8. Highlighting the Nose and Ear

```
Let video;
Let posenet;
Let pose;

Function setup() {
      createCanvas(640,480);
      video=createCapture(VIDEO);
video.hide();
posenet=m15.poseNet(video.modelready);
posenet.on('pose',showPoses);
}
```

```
Function showPoses(numberofposes) {
console.log(numberofposes);
if(numberofposes.length>0)
{
      Pose=numberofposes[0].pose;
}
}

Function modelready() {
      console.log('posenet model is ready');
}

Function draw() {
      Image(video,0,0);
      If(pose) {
fill(255,0,0);
ellipse(pose.nose.x,pose.nose.y,64);
ellipse(pose.leftEar.x.pose.leftEar.y,64);
ellipse(pose.rightEar.x.pose.rightEar.y,64);
      }
}
```

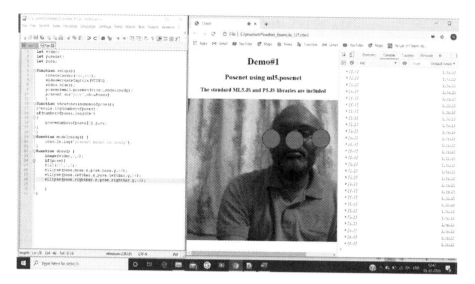

Figure 3-8. *Screenshot (output) to recognize two different poses (keypoints): nose and ear*

Step 9. Modify the draw( ) function in the 1.js script file to distinguish poses (keypoints) with multiple colors (Listing 3-9). Figure 3-9 shows the corresponding output.

Listing 3-9. Adding Multiple Colors

```
Let video;
Let posenet;
Let pose;

Function setup() {
      createCanvas(640,480);
      video=createCapture(VIDEO);
video.hide();
posenet=m15.poseNet(video.modelready);
posenet.on('pose',showPoses);
}
```

83

```
Function showPoses(numberofposes) {
console.log(numberofposes);
if(numberofposes.length>0)
{
      Pose=numberofposes[0].pose;
}
}
Function modelready() {
      console.log('posenet model is ready');
}

Function draw() {
      Image(video,0,0);
      If(pose) {
fill(255,0,0);
ellipse(pose.nose.x,pose.nose.y,64);
ellipse(pose.leftEar.x.pose.leftEar.y,32);
ellipse(pose.rightEar.x.pose.rightEar.y,32);
}
}
```

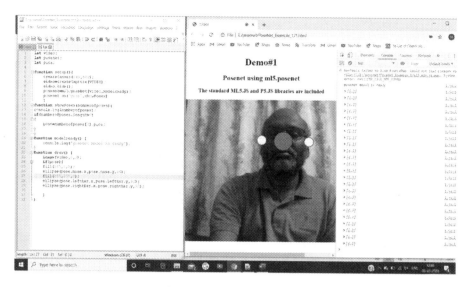

Figure 3-9. *Screenshot (output) to distinguish poses with multiple colors*

Step 10. Change the recognized poses' size and shape by modifying the instructions in the 1.js script file draw() function (Listing 3-10). Figure 3-10 shows the corresponding output.

Listing 3-10. Changing Size and Shape

```
Let video;
Let posenet;
Let pose;

Function setup() {
     createCanvas(640,480);
     video=createCapture(VIDEO);
video.hide();
posenet=m15.poseNet(video.modelready);
posenet.on('pose',showPoses);
}
```

```
Function showPoses(numberofposes) {
console.log(numberofposes);
if(numberofposes.length>0)
{
     Pose=numberofposes[0].pose;
}
}
Function modelready() {
     console.log('posenet model is ready');
}

Function draw() {
     Image(video,0,0);
     If(pose) {
fill(255,0,0);
ellipse(pose.nose.x,pose.nose.y,32);
fill(255,255,0);
ellipse(pose.leftEar.x.pose.leftEar.y,32);
ellipse(pose.rightEar.x.pose.rightEar.y,32);
let lEye=pose.leftEye;
let rEye=pose.rightEye;
let d;
d=dist(rEye.x,rEye.y,lEye.x,lEye.y);
print(d);
}
}
```

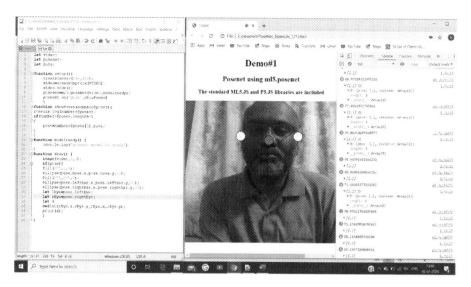

Figure 3-10. *Screenshot(output). Changing the size and shape of the recognized poses*

Step 11. Find the distance between the recognized poses by modifying the 1.js script file draw() function (Listing 3-11). Figure 3-11 shows the corresponding output.

Listing 3-11. Finding the Distance Between the Recognized Poses

```
Let video;
Let posenet;
Let pose;
Function setup() {
    createCanvas(640,480);
    video=createCapture(VIDEO);
video.hide();
posenet=m15.poseNet(video.modelready);
posenet.on('pose',showPoses);
}
```

```
Function showPoses(numberofposes) {
console.log(numberofposes);
if(numberofposes.length>0)
{
      Pose=numberofposes[0].pose;
}
}
Function modelready() {
      console.log('posenet model is ready');
}

Function draw() {
      Image(video,0,0);
      If(pose) {
fill(255,0,0);
ellipse(pose.nose.x,pose.nose.y,32);
fill(255,255,0);
ellipse(pose.leftEar.x.pose.leftEar.y,32);
ellipse(pose.rightEar.x.pose.rightEar.y,32);
let lEye=pose.leftEye;
let rEye=pose.rightEye;
let d;
d=dist(rEye.x,rEye.y,lEye.x,lEye.y);
print(d);
for (let i=0;i<pose.keypoints.length;i++) {
            let x=pose.keypoints[i].position.x;
            let y=pose.keypoints[i].position.y;
            fill(0,250,0);
            ellipse(x,y,20,20);
      }
```

```
for(let i=0;i<line_connecting_points.length;i++){
        let m=line_connecting_points[i][0];
        let n=line_connecting_points[i][1];
        strokeWeight(2);
        stroke(250);
    line(m.position.x,m.position.y,n.position.x,n.
    position.y);
    }
}
}
```

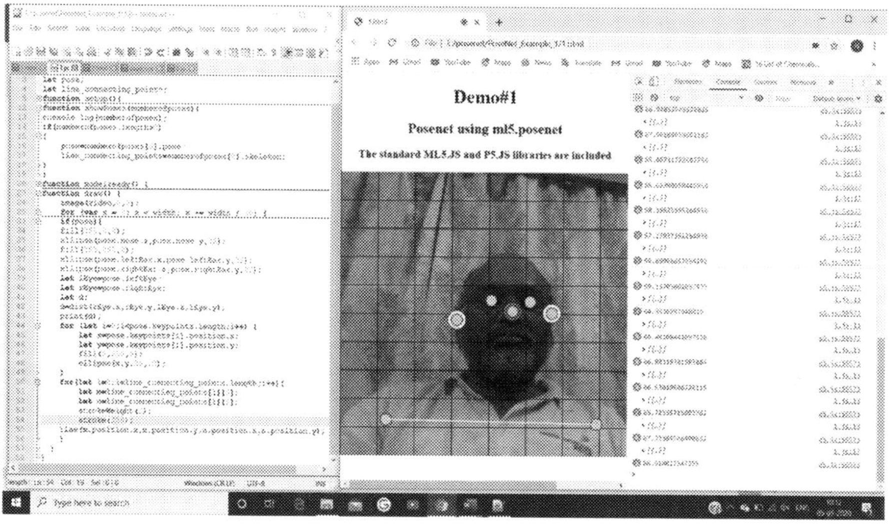

Figure 3-11. *Screenshot (output). Finding the distance between the recognized poses and displaying them on the browser console*

Now that you understand how to identify the keypoints using the PoseNet model, the focus turns to how to collect and store the data for recognizing the patterns of data through various programming structures for realizing multiple applications.

89

Input, Output, and Data Structure of the PoseNet Model

This section covers the various functions available in the program when the input is video data. This will help you to understand various functions (methods) that are available to render (load) the video on the browser and to identify the various poses whenever any movement (change) occurs.

PoseNet enables you to gauge either a solitary posture (i.e., a single pose of an individual) or various stances of multiple persons in a picture or video, which means that a rendition of the calculation can distinguish just a single individual in a picture/video and that one form can identify numerous people in a picture/video.

Input

An input, in this case, is an HTML video or an image element (picture) or a p5 image/video element of the page. If specific input is not provided, PoseNet defaults to the browser's webcam as the input. The following code snippet shows how to read the input (poses) of an individual:

```
const video = document.getElementById("video");
// Create a new myposeNet method
const myposeNet = ml5.poseNet(video, modelLoaded);

// When the model is loaded in the browser
function modelLoaded() {
  console.log("Model Loaded!");
}
```

The various parameters for the PoseNet method are as follows:

- ml5.poseNet(video[Optional], type[Optional], callback[Optional])

- ml5.poseNet(video[Optional], options[Optional], callback[Optional])

- ml5.poseNet(callback[Optional], options[Optional])

Table 3-1 describes the arguments (parameters) for the ml5.poseNet method.

Table 3-1. *ml5.poseNet Arguments*

Video (Optional)	A video element(HTML or p5)
type (**Optional**)	Estimation for single or multiple people poses.
Callback (optional)	A method to run once the model is loaded on the browser. Otherwise, a promise will be executed once the model has loaded.
Options (**optional**)	To specify the model accuracy and performance.Values to these parameters are set accordingly: imageScaleFactor, outputStride,flipHorizontal,minConfidence, maxPoseDetections,scoreThreshold, nmsRadius,detectionType,multiplier

Output

When the pose of an individual is loaded on the browser (i.e., the browser webcam reads the video stream data), the corresponding poses (keypoints) are given as the results (output) by the function poseNet(). The results (outputs) are then passed to the temporary program variable myposes, as shown here:

```
// Listen to new 'pose' events when there are changes // in the
orientation of the poses.
myposeNet.on("pose", function(results) {
  myposes = results;
});
```

.on() Function

The .on ('pose', function(results)) method triggers an event whenever a new pose is detected. The method continuously listens for a change in the poses over the video frames. The function (results) returns the results in an array of objects consisting of pose recognitions.

Summary

This chapter showed you step by step how to depict the real-time human pose estimation in the browser using Dan Oved's PoseNet model.

You learned about PoseNet model intricacies such as what a pose contains: pose confidence score, an array of 17 keypoints, and each keypoint in turn consisting of keypoint position and keypoint confidence score along with the input image space.

This chapter also covered the programming constructs required to process the collected keypoints' data. In the following chapters, you will learn about programming skills required to develop multiple applications such as human pose classifications and gait analysis.

References

https://ml5js.org/reference/api-PoseNet/

https://github.com/ml5js/ml5-library/tree/
release/src/PoseNet

https://parleylabs.com/2020/01/05/
exploration-pose-estimation-with-openpose-and-
posenet/#:~:text=PoseNet%20is%20built%20to%
20run,see%20the%20performance%20benchmarks%
20below.&text=Our%20first%20look%20was%20on,
from%20both%20OpenPose%20and%20Posenet

Toshev, A., and C. Szegedy, "DeepPose: Human
Pose Estimation via Deep Neural Networks."
2014 IEEE Conference on Computer Vision and
Pattern Recognition, pp. 1653-1660, doi: 10.1109/
CVPR.2014.214. Columbus, OH, 2014.

Tompson, J., R. Goroshin, A. Jain, Y. LeCun, and
C. Bregler, "Efficient Object Localization Using
Convolutional Networks." 2015 IEEE Conference on
Computer Vision and Pattern Recognition (CVPR),
pp. 648-656, doi: 10.1109/CVPR.2015.7298664.
Boston, MA, 2015.

Carreira, J., P. Agrawal, K. Fragkiadaki, and J. Malik,
"Human Pose Estimation with Iterative Error
Feedback." 2016 IEEE Conference on Computer
Vision and Pattern Recognition (CVPR), pp. 4733-
4742, doi: 10.1109/CVPR.2016.512. Las Vegas, NV,
2016.

Newell A., K. Yang K., and J. Deng J. "Stacked Hourglass Networks for Human Pose Estimation." In: Leibe B., J. Matas, N. Sebe, and M. Welling (eds). Computer Vision – ECCV 2016. Lecture Notes in Computer Science, vol 9912. Springer Verlag, 2016.

Xiao, Bin, Haiping Wu, and Yichen Wei. *Simple Baselines for Human Pose Estimation and Tracking.* Springer International Publishing, 2018.

https://doi.org/10.1007/978-3-030-01231-1_29, Computer Vision – ECCV 2018

Sun, K., B. Xiao, D. Liu, and J. Wang. (2019a). Deep High Resolution Representation Learning for Human Pose Estimation. In CVPR: https://openaccess.thecvf.com/content_CVPR_2019/papers/Sun_Deep_High-Resolution_Representation_Learning_for_Human_Pose_Estimation_CVPR_2019_paper.pdf

https://zhangtemplar.github.io/pose/

https://nanonets.com/blog/human-pose-estimation-2d-guide/

CHAPTER 4

Human Pose Classification

This chapter covers various human pose estimation experiments. In the preceding chapter, you learned the basics of human pose estimation in the browser.

This discussion first answers why we need human pose estimation in the browser, and then the discussion turns to various artificial intelligence (AI) and machine learning (ML) classification techniques that can be executed in the browser.

The chapter also provides a high-level overview of the open-source JavaScript (JS) library TensorFlow.js. You will learn how to use it to implement and deploy deep learning (DL) systems in browsers. The discussion covers the TensorFlow.js framework's architecture and its building-block tensors and includes two practical examples of using the library to run neural network programs on the browser. Note that TensorFlow.js is a library for ML in JS that enables you to develop ML models in JS and use ML directly in the browser or Node.js.

The chapter also includes practical examples that cover detecting the keypoints of an individual through browser webcams and locally stored pictures (images).

© Nagender Kumar Suryadevara 2021
N. K. Suryadevara, *Beginning Machine Learning in the Browser*,
https://doi.org/10.1007/978-1-4842-6843-8_4

Need for Human Pose Estimation in the Browser

Human pose estimation is one task required for an individual to assess the human pose classifications to predict the abnormalities that may arise soon. The human poses evaluation will indicate an individual's classification levels in performing his or her day-to-day activities. People prefer to have their poses computed without losing their privacy; hence, the human pose computations are preferred on the client side rather than on the server side of the data collection. So, the human pose classification (determination) with the help of AI methods is to be performed on the client side (i.e., at the browser application).

The need for ML techniques for the estimation of human poses and to evaluate the performance of the classification in the browser is as follows:

- *Privacy*: Provision for executing ML methods and the user data at the browser will ensure that data does not move to the servers. Data related to sensitive documents, medical application data such as user identification, and domain-specific user text will be processed at the client (users) end only. Thus, user privacy is maintained by implementing ML methods at the client application itself (i.e., at the browser).

- *Sharing of data (distribution) across several software not required*: The reliance of data to be executed on several software/tools can be avoided. There is no requirement to install additional software/tools. The application will be executed at the user end, and therefore navigation to several methods will be easy.

- *Low latency*: ML models can be optimized for efficient storage and speed to run on resource-constrained devices very efficiently. Therefore, wait time (round-trip time in the client/server model web application) for server responses can be lessened/avoided. Applications run faster if they execute at the client side only.

- *Reliability*: Reliability issues can be avoided because there would be no intermittent connectivity steps. The data is not transmitted to another location (server). Therefore, the data is very reliable to be processed at the client.

- *User interactivity*: Today's technological browser is integrated with the input and output devices such as cameras and screens. This integration supports rich user interactive experiences. ML can amplify user interactivity easily and, especially, in real-time operations.

Also, executing ML methods (models) on the browsers (at the client side) is appropriate for tasks such as transfer learning, parameter tuning for existing models, and output interpretation.

ML Classification Techniques in the Browser

Neural network concepts are a set of ML methods/algorithms that behave similarly to how the brain works, using an artificial neurons structure. A neural network is one of several ML methods that can help to solve classification problems. Its novel quality is in its capacity to make detailed forecasts work powerfully and to imitate human speculation within a reasonable time of execution. This chapter does not go into neural networks in detail, but you will learn the basics of neural networks so that you have a better understanding of the problems presented.

There are numerous powerful ways to classify entities automatically. Application requirements determine the ideal choice for solving classification problems and whether applying neural systems is worth the effort. Artificial neural networks (ANNs) and deep neural networks (DNNs) are successful for solving complex dimensionality issues; however, they are themselves also hypothetically complex. Some profound learning systems that are DL frameworks, such as TensorFlow, can help you set deep neural systems quicker, with just a couple of code lines.

Classification models predict the class labels such that it belongs to a particular entity. A few classifiers are paired, bringing about a yes/no choice. Others are multiclass, ready to classify a thing into one of a few classifications. Characterization is another common use case of AI. For instance, arrangement calculations are utilized to tackle email spam separating, record classification, discourse acknowledgment, picture acknowledgment, and penmanship recognition. In this specific situation, a neural system is a few AI calculations that can help take care of grouping issues. Its unique quality is its capacity to progressively make detailed forecasts and imitate human deduction, in a way that no other calculation can. Neural systems have yielded the best outcomes in numerous cases related to classification problems.

To understand classification problems with neural systems, it's necessary to figure out how other order calculations work and to understand their exceptional qualities. For some issues, a neural system might be inadmissible or pointless exercise. For other people, it may be the central arrangement. ANNs are made up of essential components called neurons, which take in value, increase it by weight, and run it through a nondirect enactment work. A neural network can learn the non-linear properties efficiently provided enough computational capabilities are existing. The system can learn exceptionally complex capacities. Hypothetically, given enough computational capabilities, a neural system can learn the state of nearly any capacity.

- *ANN Positives*: Extremely powerful for solving big dimensionality problems, ready to manage complex relations between factors, non-thorough classification sets, and complex capacities relating to yield factors. Excellent tuning alternatives to forestall over-and under-fitting.

- *ANN Shortcomings*: Hypothetically complicated, hard to actualize, and requires expertise to tune the parameters for better classification. Sometimes, require a large training set of samples for better realization (to have better output).

Note   Make your neural network and train it in the program with the TensorFlow.js library. Collect data and prepare your neural organization or utilize existing information to prepare your neural organization progressively. When it is prepared, your neural network will perform the classification or regression tasks accordingly.

Running AI/ML programs completely on the client side through a browser is an interactive application, and that is smart. Applications such as human pose estimation can be realized using the open-source JS library TensorFlow.js.

ML Using TensorFlow.js

TensorFlow.js is used to characterize, train, and run AI models totally in the browser by utilizing JS and application programming interface (API) methods. If you are a JS web developer and new to ML, TensorFlow.js is an extraordinary way to start learning and developing applications that incorporate intelligence in the browser. However, if you are an ML designer and new to JS, the material in this book will give you a speedy primer on how TensorFlow.js resources will help you develop smart applications.

While developing applications using TensorFlow.js, you might prefer one the following methods:

- You can import a pretrained model for derivation (inference). If you have a TensorFlow or Keras existing model and the model was prepared in the offline mode, you can change over into TensorFlow.js and load it into the browser for inference.

- For rapidly developing applications, the transfer learning method can be appropriate. This method allows you to use TensorFlow.js to characterize, train, and run models totally in the browser via JS and layers of API. If you are acquainted with Keras, the layers of API should be familiar to transform into a new model.

- Web developers can use TensorFlow.js to describe, train, and execute the models entirely in the browser using the JS features.

TensorFlow.js is a JS library system for AI and replaces deeplearn.js, which is presently called TensorFlow.js Core. TensorFlow.js also incorporates a Layers API, a higher-level library for building AI models that utilize Core (e.g., devices for porting TensorFlow and Keras models). Figure 4-1 shows an overview of TensorFlow.js.

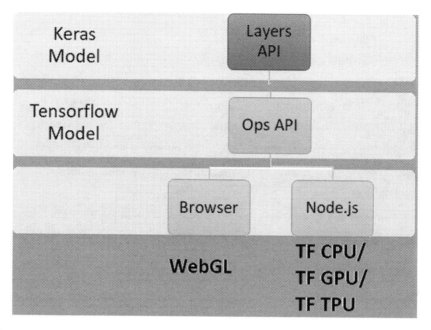

Figure 4-1. *Overview of TensorFlow.js*

You can create/build models legitimately in a browser. In addition, you can import existing previously prepared models from Python and retrain them also. If you are already working under JS stack with Not only SQL (NoSQL) and JavaScript Object Notation (JSON), a use case that you should consider is utilizing TensorFlow.js to builds models using a browser. TensorFlow.js incudes Keras API, a simple software tool used to build AI/ML learning models. It likewise incorporates a lower-level API, previously called deeplearn.js, which can be used for direct variable-based math and programmed separation. The Ops API supports eager execution. Underneath everything, TensorFlow.js is fueled by WebGL, a JS API for delivering 2D and 3D illustrations inside any Internet browser without the plug-in modules.

101

Note TensorFlow eager execution is an imperative programming environment that evaluates operations immediately, without building graphs. Instead, operations return concrete values instead of constructing a computational graph to run later. This makes it easy to get started with TensorFlow and debug models. TF CPU (central processing unit), TF GPU (graphical processing unit), and TF TPU (tensor processing unit) are the distribution strategies wherein models can be executed on the respective devices.

If there is limited information for the neural network learning process, tools such as Tensorflow are computationally efficient for better realization. Suppose there is a requirement for large data sets processing, then the Compute Unified Device Architecture (CUDA) systems such as NVIDIA GPUs/Google TPUs or Field Programmable Gate Arrays (FPGAs) are very much required. Basically, Tensorflow tools are based on JavaScript (JS) programming execution. It will support GPU for efficient data processing through WebGL API which is better than CUDA systems.

TensorFlow.js is a library for creating and preparing AI models in JS and sending them to a program or on Node.js. You can utilize existing models, convert Python TensorFlow models, use move figuring out how to retrain existing models with your information, and create models without any preparation. The TensorFlow.js Node.js condition underpins utilizing an introduced work of Python/C TensorFlow as a back end, which may utilize the machine's accessible equipment increasing speed, for instance, CUDA. There is likewise a JS-based back end for Node.js. However, its capacities are restricted. TensorFlow.js has a few back closures with various attributes. The WebGL back end provides GPU uphold utilizing WebGL surfaces for capacity and WebGL shaders for execution, and it can be up to 100x quicker than the direct CPU back end. WebGL does not need CUDA, so it can exploit whatever GPU is available.

The WebAssembly (WASM) TensorFlow.js back end for the program utilizes the XNNPACK library for upgraded CPU execution of neural organization administrators. The WASM back end is commonly a lot quicker (10x to 30x) than the JS CPU back end, but it usually is slower than the WebGL back end (aside from tiny models). Your mileage may vary, so test both the WASM and WebGL back closures for your models on your equipment.

Example: Basic usage of TensorFlow.js, consider a linear regression problem with salary and experience attributes relationship, as shown in Figure 4-2.

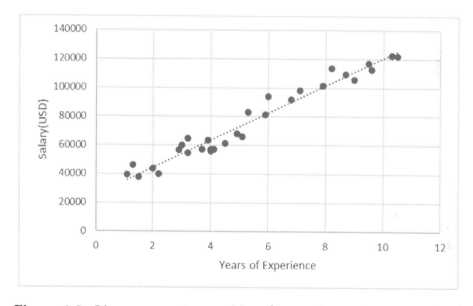

Figure 4-2. *Linear regression problem (years of experience vs. salary)*

We can infer from Figure 4-2 the y value for a particular x value even if we do not have the exact data. In ML, we can train a model based on the input data, and we do this in a browser with the help of JS features. Figure 4-3 shows the trend line and the relationship between x and y.

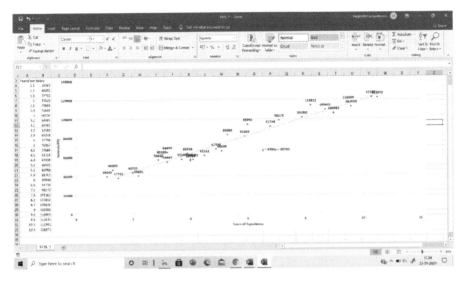

Figure 4-3. *Relationship between x and y (years of experience vs.*
salary)

Listings 4-1a and 4-1b provide the corresponding code using
TensorFlow.js to illustrate the preceding regression problem. The main file
includes the TensorFlow.js and call to the corresponding script file.

Listing 4-1a. TF_JS_1.html

```
<html>
<head>
<script src="https://cdn.jsdelivr.net/npm/@tensorflow/
tfjs@2.0.0/dist/tf.min.js">
</script>
</head>
<body>
<script src="TF_JS_1.js"></script>
      <div id="Predicted_Y_Value"></div>
</body>
</html>
```

Listing 4-1b. TF_JS_1.js

```
async function learnLinear() {
      const model= tf.sequential();
      model.add(tf.layers.dense({units: 1,inputShape: [1]}));
      model.compile({
      loss: 'meanSquaredError',
      optimizer: 'sgd'
      });
      const

      xs=tf.tensor2d([1.1,1.3,1.5,2,2.2,2.9,3,3.2,3.2,3.7,3.9,4,4,4.
1,4.5,4.9,5.1,5.3,5.9,6,6.8,7.1,7.9,8.2,8.7,9,9.5,9.6,10.3,10.5],[30
,1]);
      const
ys=tf.tensor2d([39343,46205,37731,43525,39891,56642,60150,54445,6444
5,57189,63218,55794,56957,57081,61111,67938,66029,83088,81363,93940,
91738,98273,101302,113812,109431,105582,116969,112635,122391,121872]
,[30,1]);

      await model.fit(xs,ys,{epochs: 400});
      document.getElementById('Predicted_Y_Value').
      innerText=model.predict(tf.tensor2d([11],[1,1]));
      }
learnLinear();
```

Figure 4-4 shows the screenshot (output) of the regression expression.

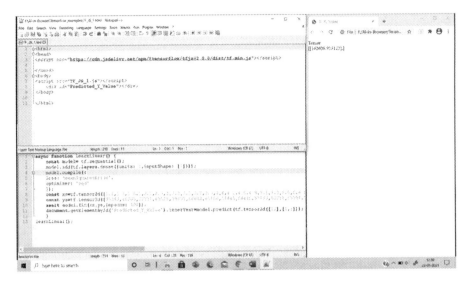

Figure 4-4. *Screenshot of the source code and the corresponding output related to the regression problem*

Changing Flat File Data into TensorFlow.js Format

Consider the iris dataset, which consists of data items with 15 samples (rows) related to various types of flowers. The iris dataset is of the JSON format, as shown in Figure 4-5. To convert the data (i.e., a flat file(Array) into TensorFlow.js format), the tf.tensor2D() function helps in creating data that TensorFlow.js can understand. The function loadJSON() in the setup() function will read the iris.json data into the model of the browser application. The browser graphical user interface (GUI) can be customized to interact with the user to the inputs such as the epochs and other parameter values.

Basically, the JSON file contains the attribute-value pair for various instances of the iris flowers. Listing 4-2a is the main file that invokes the corresponding script file consisting of operational functionalities given in Listing 4-2b.

The function setup() in the script file is responsible for setting the size of the canvas window for user interactive operations, loading the JSON data file for processing, and providing the user interactive buttons to start the model.

Loading the JSON data file contents into the user-defined temporary variables is done by the function loaddata(). The temporary data held in the user-defined variable is converted into the tensor data structures by the function convertToTensor().

After the neural network learning process is completed (i.e. after the execution of trainModel() and nn_model() functions) the model data is stored in the tensors data structure. The model gets learned with the corresponding data present in the tensors that is executed by the neural network configuration with the help of trainModel() and nn_model() functions.

```
[
{"sepalLength": 5.1, "sepalWidth": 3.5, "petalLength": 1.4, "petalWidth": 0.2, "species": "setosa"},
{"sepalLength": 4.9, "sepalWidth": 3.0, "petalLength": 1.4, "petalWidth": 0.2, "species": "setosa"},
{"sepalLength": 4.7, "sepalWidth": 3.2, "petalLength": 1.3, "petalWidth": 0.2, "species": "setosa"},
{"sepalLength": 4.6, "sepalWidth": 3.1, "petalLength": 1.5, "petalWidth": 0.2, "species": "setosa"},
{"sepalLength": 5.0, "sepalWidth": 3.6, "petalLength": 1.4, "petalWidth": 0.2, "species": "setosa"},
{"sepalLength": 5.4, "sepalWidth": 3.9, "petalLength": 1.7, "petalWidth": 0.4, "species": "setosa"},
{"sepalLength": 4.6, "sepalWidth": 3.4, "petalLength": 1.4, "petalWidth": 0.3, "species": "setosa"},
{"sepalLength": 5.0, "sepalWidth": 3.4, "petalLength": 1.5, "petalWidth": 0.2, "species": "setosa"},
{"sepalLength": 4.4, "sepalWidth": 2.9, "petalLength": 1.4, "petalWidth": 0.2, "species": "setosa"},
{"sepalLength": 4.9, "sepalWidth": 3.1, "petalLength": 1.5, "petalWidth": 0.1, "species": "setosa"},
{"sepalLength": 5.4, "sepalWidth": 3.7, "petalLength": 1.5, "petalWidth": 0.2, "species": "setosa"},
{"sepalLength": 4.8, "sepalWidth": 3.4, "petalLength": 1.6, "petalWidth": 0.2, "species": "setosa"},
{"sepalLength": 4.8, "sepalWidth": 3.0, "petalLength": 1.4, "petalWidth": 0.1, "species": "setosa"},
{"sepalLength": 4.3, "sepalWidth": 3.0, "petalLength": 1.1, "petalWidth": 0.1, "species": "setosa"},
{"sepalLength": 5.8, "sepalWidth": 4.0, "petalLength": 1.2, "petalWidth": 0.2, "species": "setosa"},
{"sepalLength": 5.7, "sepalWidth": 4.4, "petalLength": 1.5, "petalWidth": 0.4, "species": "setosa"},
{"sepalLength": 5.4, "sepalWidth": 3.9, "petalLength": 1.3, "petalWidth": 0.4, "species": "setosa"},
{"sepalLength": 5.1, "sepalWidth": 3.5, "petalLength": 1.4, "petalWidth": 0.3, "species": "setosa"},
{"sepalLength": 5.7, "sepalWidth": 3.8, "petalLength": 1.7, "petalWidth": 0.3, "species": "setosa"},
{"sepalLength": 5.1, "sepalWidth": 3.8, "petalLength": 1.5, "petalWidth": 0.3, "species": "setosa"},
{"sepalLength": 5.4, "sepalWidth": 3.4, "petalLength": 1.7, "petalWidth": 0.2, "species": "setosa"},
{"sepalLength": 5.1, "sepalWidth": 3.7, "petalLength": 1.5, "petalWidth": 0.4, "species": "setosa"},
{"sepalLength": 4.6, "sepalWidth": 3.6, "petalLength": 1.0, "petalWidth": 0.2, "species": "setosa"},
{"sepalLength": 5.1, "sepalWidth": 3.3, "petalLength": 1.7, "petalWidth": 0.5, "species": "setosa"},
```

Figure 4-5. Iris dataset in the JSON format

Note   You can download the iris.json dataset from https://www.kaggle.com/rtatman/iris-dataset-json-versio.

Listing 4-2a. TensorFlow.js. index.html function setup() to Load the .json Data

```
<!DOCTYPE html>
<html>
<head>
      <title>Iris Dataset Classification</title>
      <script src="https://cdn.jsdelivr.net/npm/@tensorflow/
      tfjs@1.0.0/dist/tf.min.js"></script>
      <script src="https://cdn.jsdelivr.net/npm/@tensorflow/
      tfjs-vis@1.0.2/dist/tfjs-vis.umd.min.js"></script>
      <script src="https://cdn.jsdelivr.net/npm/p5@1.1.9/lib/
      p5.js"></script>
      <script src="script10.js"></script>
</head>
<body>
</body>
</html>
```

Listing 4-2b. script10.js

```
let input, button
let IRIS_NUM_CLASSES =3
let nn_model;
let train_x;
let train_y;
let epoch_val;
function setup()
{
  createCanvas(710, 400);
  // Loading Data
  loadJSON('iris.json',loadData)
```

```
  // GUI Form Elements
  fill(0);
  textSize(30)
  text('Train Model',10,50)
  textSize(18)
  text('Train Epochs:',10,90)
  input = createInput();
  input.position(140, 80);
  button = createButton('Train Model From Scratch');
  button.position(20,110, 200);
  let col = color(255,127,80)
  button.style('background-color', col);
  button.size(200,40)
  button.mousePressed(greet);
 }
//The functions loaddata() and converttoTensor()to //convert
the data into tensorflow objects(tensor2D() //objects):

function loadData(data)
{
  const values = data.map(item => ({
    a: item.sepalLength,
    b: item.sepalWidth,
    c: item.petalLength,
    d: item.petalWidth,
    label: item.species
  }));

  const dataset = values.filter(item => (

    item.a != null && item.b != null && item.c != null &&
    item.d != null && item.label != null
  ));
```

```
  const {inputs, labels} = convertToTensor(dataset);
  train_x = inputs
  train_y = labels

  console.log(train_x.shape[0])
}

function convertToTensor(dataset)
{
  return tf.tidy(() => {
    tf.util.shuffle(dataset);
    const inputs = dataset.map(item => [item.a, item.b, item.c,
    item.d])
    const labels=[];
    for(i=0;i<dataset.length;i++)
    {
      if(dataset[i].label == 'setosa')
        labels.push(0)
      else if(dataset[i].label == 'versicolor')
        labels.push(1)
      else if(dataset[i].label == 'virginica')
        labels.push(2)
    }
    const inputTensor = tf.tensor2d(inputs, [inputs.length, 4]);
    const labelTensor = tf.oneHot(tf.tensor1d(labels).toInt(),
    IRIS_NUM_CLASSES);
    const inputMax = inputTensor.max();
    const inputMin = inputTensor.min();
    const normalizedInputs = inputTensor.sub(inputMin).
    div(inputMax.sub(inputMin));
    return {
      inputs: normalizedInputs,
      labels: labelTensor,
```

```
// Return the min/max bounds so we can use them //later.
     inputMax,
     inputMin,
   }
 });
}

//Function iris_nn_model() to invoke the //createmodel()and
train the neural network model
function iris_nn_model()
{
     epoch_val = int(input.value())

     if(epoch_val>0)
     {
          nn_model = createModel()
          tfvis.show.modelSummary({name: 'Model Summary'},
          nn_model);

          if(train_x.shape[0] >0 && train_y.shape[0] >0 )
               trainModel(nn_model)
     }
}
// Function createModel() tf.sequential(),adding //input layers
through tf.layers.dense and //trainModel() with the model.fit()
methods
function createModel()
{
  const model = tf.sequential();
  model.add(tf.layers.dense({inputShape: [4], units: 50,
  useBias: true, activation:'relu'}));
  model.add(tf.layers.dense({units: 20, activation: 'relu'}));
```

```
//model.add(tf.layers.dense({units: 10, activation: 'relu'}));
model.add(tf.layers.dense({units: 3, activation: 'softmax'}));
return model;
}

async function trainModel(model)
{
    model.compile({
      optimizer: tf.train.adam(),
      loss: tf.losses.softmaxCrossEntropy,
      metrics: ['accuracy'],
    });
  const batchSize = 32;
   const epochs = epoch_val;
   const validationSplit =0.3;
   return await model.fit(train_x, train_y, {
     batchSize,
     epochs,
     validationSplit,
     shuffle: true,
     callbacks: tfvis.show.fitCallbacks(
        { name: 'Training Performance' },
        ['loss', 'val_loss','acc','val_acc'],
        { height: 200, callbacks: ['onEpochEnd'] })
    });
}
```

Figure 4-6 shows the output related to the training process and the epoch accuracy using the TensorFlow.js visualization.

Figure 4-6. *Screenshot(output) for the input read from the JSON file*

Artificial Neural Network Model in the Browser Using TensorFlow.js

1. Load or prepare the data.

2. Set your neural network structure.

3. Add configuration information to the neural network.

4. Train your neural organization.

5. Utilize the prepared model to make an order.

6. Accomplish something (classification/predicting) with the outcomes obtained.

The next section provides a brief description of a simple neural network and then covers the intricacies of developing an ANN through TensorFlow.js programming principles.

Trivial Neural Network

Consider the neural network organization consisting of one hidden layer
for the function y(output)=x' (inverse of x) with four neurons in the hidden
layer, two neurons in the input layer, and one neuron in the output layer,
where x is the set of inputs (see Figure 4-7).

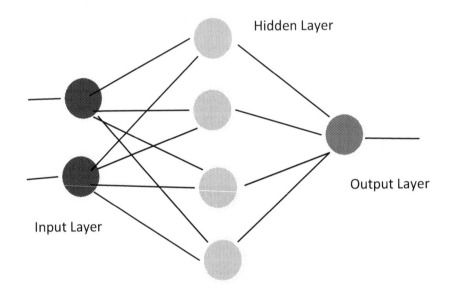

Figure 4-7. *Basic structure of an ANN*

Building neural structures is typically done by stacking layers.
TensorFlow.js gives an API to stack various sorts of layers. The number of
various parameters to be considered for configuration is more than you
anticipate. One reason is that this model incorporates weight and bias values.
For the time being, you can consider the inclinations from one layer to
another through the parameters that encourage you to improve models. The
errors continue to be lessened all through the process of training; it implies
that our model is getting learned.

Example 1: Neural Network Model in TensorFlow.js

Listing 4-3a is in the main index file, and Listing 4-3b is the script file that includes the data structures to hold the data in the tensors, setup, and configuration of the neural network model to realize the functionality of the inverse operation.

Listing 4-3a. Demo1.html (Main File)

```
<!DOCTYPE html>
<html>
<head>
  <title>A simple Neural Network model </title>
  <!-- Import TensorFlow.js -->
  <script src="https://cdn.jsdelivr.net/npm/@tensorflow/
  tfjs@1.0.0/dist/tf.min.js"></script>
   <!-- Import the main script file -->
  <script src="script.js"></script>
</head>
<body>
<h2> Neural Network to demonstrate y=x' (Y is equal to inverse
of X)
</body>
</html>
```

Listing 4-3b. Script.js (Script File)

```
//Step 1:load data, xs=Input and ys=Output
const xs=tf.tensor2d([[0,0],[0.5,0.5],[1,1]]);
const ys=tf.tensor2d([[1],[0.5],[0]]);

//Step 2: Set your neural network structure
const model =tf.sequential();
```

```
const confighidden={
      inputShape:[2],
      units:4,
      activation:'sigmoid'
}

const configoutput={
      units:1,
      activation:'sigmoid'
}

const hidden =tf.layers.dense(confighidden);
const output=tf.layers.dense(configoutput);

model.add(hidden);
model.add(output);

//Step 3: add configuration information
const sgdopt=tf.train.sgd(0.1);

const config={
      optimizer:sgdopt,
      loss:'meanSquaredError'
}
//Step 4: Train your neural organization
model.compile(config);

async function train()
{
      for(let i=0;i<5000;i++) {
const response=await model.fit(xs,ys);
console.log(response.history.loss[0]);
} }
```

Step 5 and 6: Utilize the results (prediction)

```
train().then(() => {
    let outputs=model.predict(xs);
    outputs.print();
    console.log('training complete');
});
```

Figure 4-8 shows the browser console's output for the preceding code.

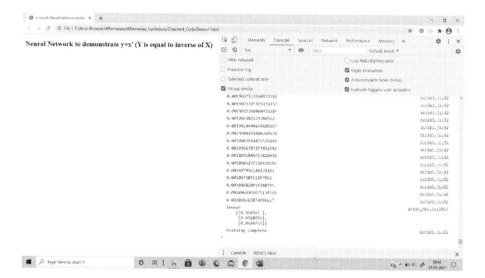

Figure 4-8. *Screenshot (output) for the y=x' through ANN using TensorFlow.js*

Example 2: A Simple ANN to Realize the "Not AND" (NAND) Boolean Operation

Not AND (NAND) Boolean operation rules are simple: Given two Boolean values (true/false), if only both are true, then return false; otherwise, return true. The neural network to realize this operation based on the input values can be demonstrated in applying a sequential model with the TensorFlow.js script library.

117

Figure 4-9 shows the basic logical NAND operation, and its corresponding functionality is shown in the truth table.

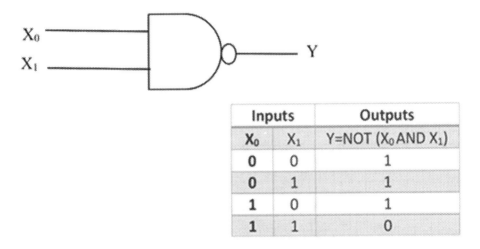

Inputs		Outputs
X_0	X_1	Y=NOT (X_0 AND X_1)
0	0	1
0	1	1
1	0	1
1	1	0

Figure 4-9. *Basic logical NAND gate and its truth table*

The training data for the NAND Boolean operation realization is by using two arrays, one for the inputs (X0 and X1) and the other for outputs (Y). The two arrays are the tensors that can be used in the neural network structure:

```
//Step 1: Load or prepare the data
const xs=tf.tensor2d([[0,0],[0,1],[1,0],[1,1]],[4,2]);
const ys=tf.oneHot(tf.tensor1d([1,1,1,0]).toInt(),2);
```

So, the shape of the input array is [4,2] because there is an array of 4 values and each array has 2 values. It would be better mentioning the arrays (input and output) with the appropriate TensorFlow.js functions.

Once the inputs and outputs are defined, the neural system can be structured in the form of layers. As the data moves forward in one direction from the input layer to the output layer, we can consider a *sequential model* for the neural system structure, as given in the previous example. The input consisting of X0 and X1 is passed on to the next layer (hidden), which consists of 5 neurons. They are then passed to the output layer consisting of 2 neurons, which shows us the certainty percentage (a value between 1 and 0) of the related outputs (true or false):

```
//Step 2: Set up the NN structure
const model =tf.sequential();

const confighidden={
      inputShape:[2],
      units:5,
      activation:'sigmoid'
}

const configoutput={
      units:2,
      activation:'sigmoid'
}

const hidden =tf.layers.dense(confighidden);
const output=tf.layers.dense(configoutput);

model.add(hidden);
model.add(output);
```

The neural network model can be trained with the optimizer function Adam along with the loss function of categoricalCrossentropy. This will enable the model to train by correlating the given input values with the corresponding output values:

```
//Step 3: Add configuration parameters to the NN //structure
const admopt=tf.train.adam(0.1);

const config={
      optimizer:admopt,
      loss:'categoricalCrossentropy' }
//Step 4: Train the NN organization
model.compile(config);
```

The training is performed by the .fit() function of the model object. This method receives the XS and YS training data and the configuration object. The config includes epochs. The .fit() method returns a promise function when the model gets to train. The output data is retrieved by calling the async call to the training method:

```
async function train()
{
        for(let i=0;i<200;i++) {
const response=await model.fit(xs,ys);
console.log(response.history.loss[0]);
} }
//Steps 5 and 6: Collect the results
train().then(() => {
        let outputs=model.predict(xs);
        outputs.print();
        console.log('training complete');
});
```

```
The output:
Tensor
    [[0, 1],
     [0.0004133, 0.9995866],
     [0.0004822 , 0.9995178],
     [0.9984748, 0.0015252]]
```

In this example, for the inputs of [0,0],[0,1] and [1,0], the predicted outputs are [0, 1] , [0.0004153, 0.9995866] and [0.0004822 , 0.9995178] implies that 0.0% certainty of FALSE and a 99.9% certainty of TRUE; whereas for the input [1,1], the output is [0.9984748, 0.0015252 implies 99% FALSE and 0.0% TRUE.

Figure 4-10 shows the output in the browser console for the preceding code.

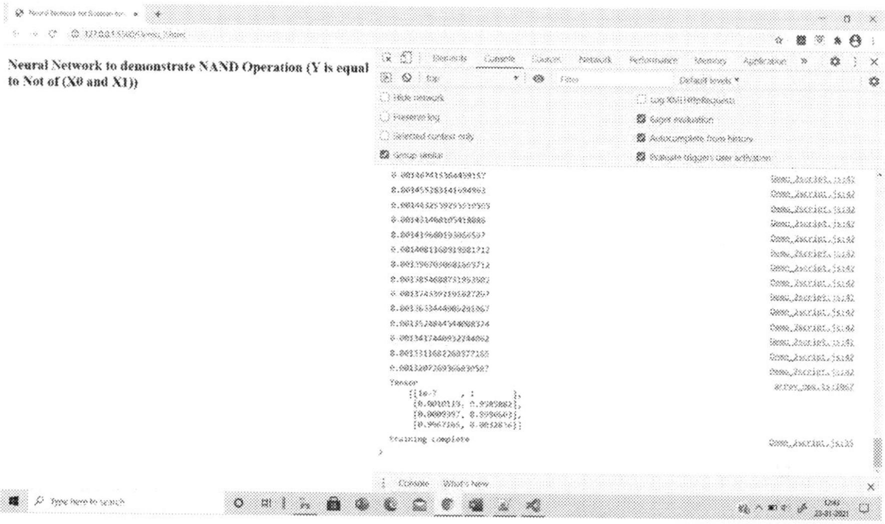

Figure 4-10. *Screenshot (output) for the NAND Boolean operation through ANN using TensorFlow.js*

Human Pose Classification Using PoseNet

"PoseNet is a vision model" that can be used to gauge the posture of an individual in a picture or video by assessing where key body joints are located. See Figure 4-11 for model terminology.

PoseNet does not perceive who is in a picture/video. The estimation is virtually assessing where human key body joints are located. PoseNet can be used to assess either a single person's posture or numerous stances of people present in a picture/video. The estimation of PoseNet can distinguish just a single individual in a picture/video and can also recognize different people in a picture/video. The single-person posture identifier is quicker and more straightforward, but requires just one subject be present in the picture. The posture assessment occurs in two stages:

1. An information RGB picture is taken care of through a convolutional neural system.

2. Posture estimation is utilized to interpret keypoint positions and keypoint certainty scores from the model's output.

Terminology related to Posenet model

Pose —PoseNet will estimate the posture object that contains a rundown of keypoints and an occurrence level certainty score for the identified individual in the picture/video.

Pose Confidence score — this decides the general trust in the assessment of a posture. It ranges somewhere in the range of 0.0 and 1.0.

Keypoint — an aspect of an individual's represent that is assessed, for example, the nose, right ear, left knee, right foot, and so forth. It contains both a position and a keypoint certainty score. PoseNet as of now distinguishes 17 keypoints.

Keypoint Confidence Score — this decides the certainty that an expected keypoint position is exact. It ranges somewhere in the range of 0.0 and 1.0

Keypoint Position — 2-Dimensional x and y facilitates in the first information picture where a keypoint has been identified.

The key points detected are indexed by "ID and Part", with a confidence score between 0.0 and 1.0, 1.0 being the highest.

Id	Part
0	nose
1	leftEye
2	rightEye
3	leftEar
4	rightEar
5	leftShoulder
6	rightShoulder
7	leftElbow
8	rightElbow
9	leftWrist
10	rightWrist
11	leftHip
12	rightHip
13	leftKnee
14	rightKnee
15	leftAnkle
16	rightAnkle

Figure 4-11. *Terminology related to PoseNet model*

Setting Up a PoseNet Project

Step 1: Including TensorFlow.js and PoseNet Libraries in the HTML Program (Main File)

```html
<html>
  <body>
    <!-- Load TensorFlow.js -->
    <script src="https://unpkg.com/@tensorflow/tfjs"></script>
    <!-- Load Posenet -->
    <script src="https://unpkg.com/@tensorflow-models/posenet">
    </script>
    <script type="text/javascript">
      posenet.load().then(function(net) {
        // posenet model loaded
      });
    </script>
  </body>
</html>
```

Figure 4-12 shows the inclusion of library files in the main file and the corresponding output in the browser. ml5.js, along with TensorFlow. js, gives the PoseNet model. A ready-to-use model that has a previously prepared convolutional neural network (CNN) inside it accepts a picture as information and yields a keypoint heatmap and the corresponding vectors.

Figure 4-12. *Output text rendered on the browser and its console window as shown after the libraries are loaded in the browser*

Step 2: Single-Person Pose Estimation Using a Browser Webcam

There are two files for the complete code: Demo_3.html (the main web page to display the output) and Demo_3script.js (the JS code to capture user video). Demo_3.html is the main page to display the output with the keypoints. Because of this, the libraries are added in this file:

```html
<html>
<head>
<title> Demo on Posenet Model </title>
<script src="p5.min.js"></script>
<script src="p5.dom.min.js"></script>
<script src="ml5.min.js" type="text/javascript"></script>
</head>
<body>
<h2> Demo of PoseNet ML model in the browser</h2>
<p id='uservideo'> Loading Model....</p>
<script src="Demo_3script.js"> </script>
</body>
</html>
```

The Demo3_script.js consists of three methods (functions):

1. function setup(): The initial setup to capture
    video using browser webcam and set the user video
    at the said location by calling the PoseNet model.
    This first function is executed and runs exactly once.

```
function setup() {
        createCanvas(640,480);
        webcam_output=createCapture(VIDEO);
        webcam_output.size=(width,height);
        myposenet=ml5.poseNet(webcam_output,function(){
        select('#uservideo').html('User Video Loaded')});
        myposenet.on('pose',function(results) {
        poses=results; });
        webcam_output.hide();
}
```

createCanvas(width, height) of the p5.js library
is to create a window (box) in the browser to display
the output. The size of the window (canvas) is set
with width:640px and height:480px.

createCapture(VIDEO) is used to capture a webcam
feed video and return a p5 object, which is stored
in the user-defined variable webcam_output. The
webcam video is also the same height and width as
the canvas.

poseNet() method creates a new PoseNet model,
taken as input from the webcam_output, and loaded
into the main .html page to display the user video.

poseNet.on() method is an event listener.
Whenever a change occurs in the user position/
video, a new image is given to the myposenet
model. The function poseNet, in turn, calls the
function(results) where the model gives the
keypoints and their corresponding scores. The
results are stored in the array named poses.

The function webcam_output.hide(), hides the
actual webcam output, and only the canvas with the
keypoints as output is displayed on the browser.

2. function draw (): The function is called and
   repeats forever until the browser is closed. This
   method in turn calls to identify the keypoints:

```
function draw() {
        image(webcam_output,0,0,width,height);
        displayKeypoints();
}
```

The draw () function continuously runs to display
the image in the canvas. It has five parameters,
the webcam_output (video to be displayed), xy
coordinates of the upper-left corner in relation to
the canvas, and width,height to draw the video.
This function calls the displayKeypoints() to
display the recognized keypoints as dots (ellipses).

3. function displayKeypoints(): This method
   displays the recognized keypoints from the array
   poses. The identified points are displayed in the
   form of circles to show that there is a keypoint:

```
function displayKeypoints() {
 for(let i=0;i<poses.length;i++) {
      let pose=poses[i].pose;
      for(let j=0;j<pose.keypoints.length;j++) {
      let point=pose.keypoints[j];
      fill(0,0,255);
      noStroke();
 ellipse(point.position.x,point.position.y,10,10);
             }
        }
 }
```

Figure 4-13 shows the corresponding output.

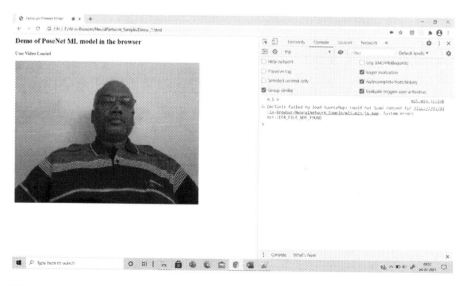

Figure 4-13. *Single-person pose estimation using a browser webcam*

Single-person pose estimation using a picture: The function setup()
consists of a createImg method to load the image (picture) from the local
hard disk onto the browser for recognizing the keypoints on the image.
Figure 4-14 shows the corresponding output.

The following set of instructions in the functions are to be written in Demo_4script.js. The main file Demo_4.html remains the same:

```
function setup() {
  createCanvas(640, 360);
  img= createImg('pics/pexels-derick-santos-2773934.jpg');
  img.size(width, height);
  myposenet = ml5.poseNet(img, function(){
  select('#userpic').html('Image Loaded');
  myposenet.singlePose(img);}};
  myposenet.on('pose', function (results) {
      poses = results; });
}
```

The function draw() contains the methods to display the keypoints and also to display the skeleton (sketch related to the joining of keypoints) based on the poses array:

```
function draw() {
    if (poses.length > 0) {
        image(img, 0, 0, width, height);
        displayKeypoints(poses);
        displaySkeleton(poses);
    }
}
```

The logic of the displayKeypoints remains the same as discussed in the previous example. The function displaySkeleton() is to draw the *lines* on the current image. draw() does this in an infinite loop, hence showing a continuous output to the user.

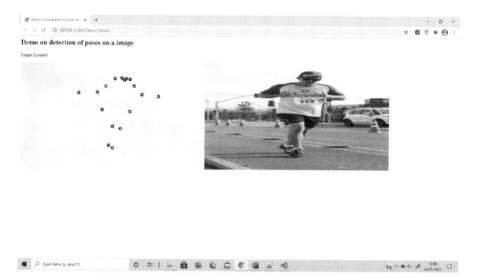

Figure 4-14. *Display of keypoints from a picture*

PoseNet Model Confidence Values

The draw function executes and loops through every keypoint that is part of the body, and the keypoints array poses contains the following information:

> "part": The name of the body part recognized.
>
> "position.x" and "position.y": Values of a point in the image.
>
> "score": Confidence value indicates the accuracy of detection.

Figure 4-15 shows the output on the browser console.

Figure 4-15. *Confidence values as seen from the poses in the browser console*

We can draw a point if the detection accuracy is greater than a certain value (e.g., 0.2 or 0.3, or 0.7 and above when you are concerned about certain points). Figure 4-16 shows the scores related to the drawn skeleton.

Figure 4-16. *Scores of certain threshold values as seen in the poses object on the browser console*

Note   When storing data using the JSON format related to output of the PoseNet model, steps are to be written in Demo_4script.js. The main file Demo_4.html remains the same

---

To capture the keypoint onto a separate file in terms of JSON format, you can use the p5 library functions as follows:

Step 1. Declare a global variable:

```
let writer;
```

Step 2. In the setup function, initialize the writer variable with the createWriter along with the file name for storing the data in the JSON format:

```
// writer object is initialized with createWriter function
writer=createWriter('data_keypoints.json');
```

Step 3. In the displayKeypoints method, invoke the function print by using the writer object:

```
writer.print("keypoint: "+keypoint.part+" x:"+keypoint.
position.x+" y:"+keypoint.position.y);
```

Step 4. Define a function for an event to occur such as mouseclick, so that the event will trigger the print method to store the values of the continuous draw() method:

```
function mouseClicked() {
        writer.close();
    }
```

The output is stored in a .json file, as shown in Figure 4-17.

Figure 4-17. *Storage of key points data in the .json file*

Summary

This chapter covered the importance of ANN and its strategies in ML modeling for human pose estimation. Through theory and examples in this chapter, you learned the basics of ANN and how to realize it in the browser through TensorFlow.js programming. Such an understanding will certainly help you to implement various ML models such as PoseNet in the browser.

PoseNet model as presented in the chapter is an Machine Learning model that estimates human pose key-points in real-time on a browser. The corresponding implementation details are presented in this chapter.

This information will serve as the basis to perform complex data analysis on the browser (as you will learn in the following chapters).

References

https://medium.com/tensorflow/real-time-human-pose-estimation-in-the-browser-with-tensorflow-js-7dd0bc881cd5

https://js.tensorflow.org/api/latest/

https://github.com/topics/neural-network

https://github.com/tensorflow/tfjs-models/tree/master/posenet

https://codelabs.developers.google.com/codelabs/neural-tensorflow-js/index.html?index=..%2F..index#0

https://rubikscode.net/2019/03/25/image-classification-with-tensorflow-js/

https://p5js.org/reference/#/p5/createWriter

https://www.smashingmagazine.com/2019/09/machine-learning-front-end-developers-tensorflowjs/

https://www.pexels.com/search/running/

https://www.pexels.com/search/jogging/

https://frl.nyu.edu/pose-estimation-in-javascript-with-tensorflow-js/

https://www.irenealvarado.com/tensorflowjs-posenet

https://learn.ml5js.org/docs/#/reference/neural-network

https://becominghuman.ai/machine-learning-in-the-browser-using-tensorflow-js-3e453ef2c68c

CHAPTER 5

Gait Analysis

Gait analysis refers to the systematic study of animal locomotion, more specifically the study of human motion, using the eye and the brain of observers augmented by instrumentation to measure body movements, body mechanics, and muscle activity. Gait analysis is used to assess and treat people with medical conditions that affect their ability to walk.

Gait analysis envelopes the measurements (presentation and investigation of quantifiable boundaries of walks) and interpretation from the person's gait patterns.

Gait Measurement Techniques

Gait analysis involves measurement, where measurable parameters are introduced, analyzed, and interpreted to conclude the subject's walking styles (patterns). Table 5-1 describes pressure measurements, and Table 5-2 identifies motion measurements.

Table 5-1. *Using Force/Pressure Measurements*

Type of Devices	Types of Measurements	
Foot switches	cadence, timing	
Glass plate views	Pressure distribution	
Pressure plates	Pressure distribution	
Pressure insoles	Pressure distribution inside a shoe	
Force plates	Net force, centre of pressure	

© Nagender Kumar Suryadevara 2021
N. K. Suryadevara, *Beginning Machine Learning in the Browser*,
https://doi.org/10.1007/978-1-4842-6843-8_5

Table 5-2. *Motion Measurements*

Device Type	Measurement Type
Goniometers	Range of motion
Electro goniometers	Joint angle at successive instants
Observational gait analysis: Conductive walkway using video cameras	Stride length, cadence, velocity, and dynamic base
High-speed video	Stop-motion measurements
Accelerometers	Accelerations
Gyroscopes	Change in orientation
3D marker systems	All possible kinematic measures using • Passive (reflectors) and active (lights) • Markers on landmarks (joint angles by "connecting the dots")
Electromagnetic field	All possible kinematic measures Noisy and qualitative Indicator of when the muscle is active Surface Electromyography (sEMG) (most common): Cheap, easy Difficult to interpret because of crosstalk and noise Fine-wire and needle EMG: Penetrate skin Isolate single muscle

Note   With regard to the observational gait analysis, the conductive walkway using video camera technique is considered in this book to analyze the individual's gait patterns using a low-cost resource-constrained computing device such as Raspberry Pi or mobile device. For understanding, the programs can be run using a laptop browser.

Gait Cycle Measurement Parameters and Terminology

Table 5-3 provides the basic terminology and the normal conditions of the gait cycle measurements. To understand an individual's walking patterns through the artificial intelligence (AI) in a browser, the following conditions will be considered for the normal gait patterns.

Table 5-3. *Basic Gait Cycle Terminiology*

Gait Cycle (Synonym)	Stride
Definition	The fundamental unit to describe the gait (i.e., the period from the time that the heel contacts the ground to the time that the same heel contacts the ground again)
Operational definition	The duration from heel strike of one foot to heel strike of the same foot
Normal gait cycle consist of two phases:	
Stance Phase (60%)	Swing Phase (40%)
Heel Strike	Toe Off	Heel Strike
Stance phase	Heel strike on the ground → toe off Contact period, midstance period, and propulsive period
Swing phase	Toe off → heel strike on the ground Acceleration, mid-swing and deceleration
Step length	Average step length = 35.41cm
Stride length	Average stride length = 70.82cm
Cadence	Average cadence = 111 steps/min
Velocity	Average walking speed = 82m/min

The design and development of the graphical user interface (GUI) through a browser in the following section will enable us to measure the gait parameters of an individual.

Web User Interface for Monitoring Gait Parameters

Figure 5-1 shows the initial output of the keypoints, skeleton, and the gait parameter values using the PoseNet model with the help of the ml5.js library.

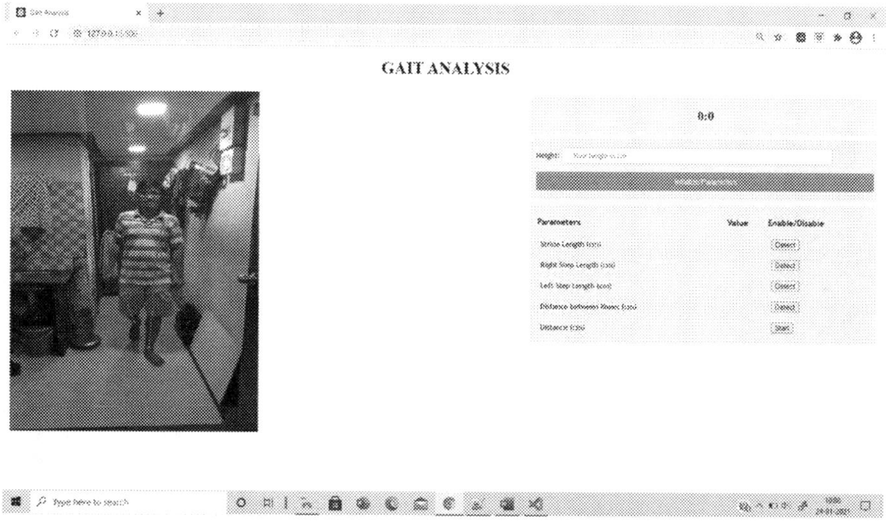

Figure 5-1. *Monitoring of gait parameters on the browser*

The source code consists of the following two files:

index.html: The main page to show output, as shown in Figure 5-1

video-script.js: Our JavaScript (JS) code running using ml5 library functions

Figure 5-2 shows the corresponding source code screenshot in the Visual Studio Code.

Figure 5-2. *Screenshot of gait parameter monitoring source code*

index.html

This is the front page to display the output (PoseNet skeleton and the measures parameters). The library ml5.js is added using the script tag in the head section of the index.html file:

```
<script src="https://unpkg.com/ml5@0.4.3/dist/ml5.min.js">
</script>
```

The front page of the user interface is defined in the body section of the HTML file. Our own JS code is inside the body. Run the index.html file in the Visual Studio Code to see the output (Listing 5-1).

Note   The developed program takes the input from a recorded video file. If the user wants to provide the input from the browser webcam, the steps given in Chapter 4 apply to collecting user data.

Listing 5-1. The body Section of the index.html File

```
<body>
    <h1 id="heading">GAIT ANALYSIS</h1>
      <div id="container-1">
        <canvas id="pose-canvas"></canvas>
        <video id="pose-video" loop muted> </video>
      </div>
      <div id="container-2">
          <div id="block-1">
          <h2 id="time">0:0</h3>
           </div>
          <div id="block-2">
            <label for="height">Height:</label>
             <input type="text" id="height" name="height"
             placeholder="Your height in cm.."><br>
             <button type="button" id="bttn3">Initialize
             Parameters</button>
          </div>
      <table id="block-3">
       <tr>
         <th>Parameters</th>
         <th>Value</th>
         <th>Enable/Disable</th>
       </tr>
       <tr>
         <td>Stride Length (cm)</td>
         <td id="stride"></td>
         <td><button id="bttn4" type="button">Detect
         </button></td>
       </tr>
       <tr>
```

```
            <td>Right Step Length (cm)</td>
            <td id="rs-d"></td>
            <td><button id="bttn5" type="button">Detect</button>
            </td> </tr>

      <tr>
       <td>Left Step Length (cm)</td>
       <td id="ls-d"></td>
       <td><button id="bttn6" type="button">Detect</button></td>
      </tr>
      <tr>
        <td>Distance between Knees (cm)</td>
        <td id="knee-d"></td>
        <td><button id="bttn7" type="button">Detect</button></td>
      </tr>
      <tr>
       <td>Distance (cm)</td>
       <td id="distance"></td>
       <td><button id="bttn8"type="button">Start</button></td>
      </tr>
    </table>
    </div>
    <script src="video-script.js"> </script>
    </body>
```

Figure 5-3 shows the initial output when the program is run on the browser.

Figure 5-3. *Initial output. The user has to enter the height value and click appropriate buttons to view the gait parameters*

The head section of the index.html consists of Cascading Style Sheets (CSS) styles for the front page of the web interface (Listing 5-2).

Listing 5-2. The head Section of the index.html file

```
<head>
     <style>
         #heading{
             text-align: center;
         }
         #pose-canvas{
             position: absolute;
         }
         #pose-video{
             display: none;
         }
         #container-1{
             float: left;
```

143

```
        width: 50%;
        padding: 5px;
    }
    #container-2{
        float: right;
        width: 40%;
        padding: 5px;
    }
    #block-1{
        text-align: center;
        border-radius: 5px;
        background-color: #f2f2f2;
        padding: 1px;
        margin: 8px 0;
    }
    #block-2{
        border-radius: 5px;
        background-color: #f2f2f2;
        padding: 10px;
    }
    #block-2 input[type=text] {
        width: 80%;
        padding: 6px 20px;
        margin: 8px 0;
        display: inline-block;
        border: 1px solid #ccc;
        border-radius: 4px;
        box-sizing: border-box;
    }
    #block-2 button{
        width: 100%;
        background-color: #4CAF50;
```

```
    color: white;
    padding: 10px 20px;
    margin: 8px 0;
    border: none;
    border-radius: 4px;
    cursor: pointer;
}
#block-2 label{
    font-family: "Trebuchet MS", Arial, Helvetica,
    sans-serif;
    font-size: 14px;
}
#block-3{
    font-family: "Trebuchet MS", Arial, Helvetica,
    sans-serif;
    width: 100%;
    margin: 8px 0;
    border-radius: 5px;
    background-color: #f2f2f2;
    padding: 10px;
}
#block-3 td, #gait-details th {
    padding: 8px;
}
#block-3 td{
    font-size: 14px;
}
#block-3 th{
    padding-top: 12px;
    padding-bottom: 12px;
```

```
                text-align: left;
            }
        </style>
<title>Gait Analysis</title>
<link rel="icon" type="image/png" href="img/uoh.png">
<script src="https://unpkg.com/ml5@0.4.3/dist/ml5.min.js">
</script>
</head>
```

The Video-script.js file that follows consists of these functions:

- async function main(): This function is executed and runs only once. When the user interacts by clicking the buttons to read the respective values from the video file, the initial setup is done here. The width and height of the video file are initialized. ml5.poseNet() creates a new PoseNet model, taking as input from the video file.

- function modelReady():Invokes the draw() function to identify the keypoints after the video file is read. video.play() function repeatedly plays the video file.

- function draw(): This function loop forever.invoke the drawImage() function to display the video image by image with the width, height, x-position, y-position, and the video to display. The keypoints and the skeleton to draw the dots and the lines on the current image. As the draw() does this in an infinite loop, it shows the user's continuous output, which makes it look like a video.

- The measurements (for the keypoints) identified for walking a certain distance are measured with the help of the positions of the video's keypoints.

- function `document.addEventListener()`: Appends an event listener for events whose type attribute value is type. The `callback` argument sets the callback that will be invoked when the event is dispatched. The callback function is the `main()` function.

```
async function main()
{
const initializeBttn = document.getElementById("bttn3");
const strideBttn = document.getElementById("bttn4");
const rightStepBttn = document.getElementById("bttn5");
const leftStepBttn = document.getElementById("bttn6");
const kneeBttn = document.getElementById("bttn7")
const distanceBttn = document.getElementById("bttn8");

    initializeBttn.onclick = function(){
        initializeParameters(initializeBttn)
    }
// when the user clicks the buttons, appropriate //method is
invoked
    strideBttn.onclick = function(){
        toggleStrideLength(strideBttn)
    }

    rightStepBttn.onclick = function(){
        toggleRightStep(rightStepBttn)
    }

    leftStepBttn.onclick = function(){
        toggleLeftStep(leftStepBttn)
    }
```

```
kneeBttn.onclick = function(){
        toggleKnee(kneeBttn)
    }

    distanceBttn.onclick = function(){
        toggleDistance(distanceBttn)
    }

const options = {
        imageScaleFactor: 0.3,
        outputStride: 16,
        flipHorizontal: false,
        minConfidence: 0.5,
        maxPoseDetections: 2,
        scoreThreshold: 0.5,
        nmsRadius: 20,
        detectionType: 'multiple',
        multiplier: 0.75,
    }

    video.src = "videos/video5.mp4"; // video File

    video.width = conFigure video.width;
    video.height= conFigure video.height;

    canvas.width = conFigure video.width;
    canvas.height = conFigure video.height;
    console.log("Canvas initialized");

const poseNet = ml5.poseNet(video,options, modelReady);
    poseNet.on('pose',gotPoses);
}
```

```
function modelReady()
{
    console.log('Model Ready')
    video.play();
    draw();
}

function draw()
{
    if (video.paused || video.ended) {
        return;
    }
    ctx.drawImage(video,0, 0, video.width, video.height)
//For each pose, measure the distance between the //respective
keypoints of the body part.
    if(pose)
    {
     for(i=0;i< pose.pose.keypoints.length;i++)
        {
            let x = pose.pose.keypoints[i].position.x;
             let y = pose.pose.keypoints[i].position.y
            drawPoint(x,y,3,'red')
        }
        let skeleton = pose.skeleton
        for(i=0;i<skeleton.length;i++)
        {
            let partA = skeleton[i][0];
            let partB = skeleton[i][1];
            drawLine(partA.position.x, partA.position.y, partB.
            position.x, partB.position.y,'red')
        }
```

```
let ankleL = pose.pose.leftAnkle
let ankleR = pose.pose.rightAnkle
let kneeL = pose.pose.leftKnee
let kneeR = pose.pose.rightKnee

if(dflag)
{
    let end_point = (ankleL.y+ankleR.y)/2
    let d = Math.abs(start_point - end_point)
    d = (height_cm / height_px) * d
document.getElementById("distance").innerHTML = d.toFixed(2)
}

if(kflag == true)
{
    let d = distance(kneeL.x, kneeL.y, kneeR.x,
    kneeR.y)
    d = (height_cm / height_px) * d
    document.getElementById("knee-d").innerHTML=
    d.toFixed(2);
}

if(rsflag == true)
{
    let d = ankleR.y - ankleL.y
    d = (height_cm / height_px) * d

    if (d <= lr_step_threshold)
    {
document.getElementById("rs-d").innerHTML = 0;
    }
```

```
        else
        {
    document.getElementById("rs-d").innerHTML = (d-lr_step_
    threshold).toFixed(2);
            n1=d;
        }
     }

     if(lsflag == true)
     {
         let d = ankleL.y - ankleR.y
         d = (height_cm / height_px) * d

         if (d <= lr_step_threshold)
         {
    document.getElementById("ls-d").innerHTML = 0;
         }
         else
         {
    document.getElementById("ls-d").innerHTML = (d- lr_step_
    threshold).toFixed(2);
            n2=d;
         }
     }
     if(strideflag == true)
     {
         if( n1 > 0 && n2 > 0 )
document.getElementById("stride").innerHTML = (n1+n2).
toFixed(2)
         else
document.getElementById("stride").innerHTML = "Unable to detect
feet";
```

```
        }
    }

    requestAnimationFrame(draw);
}
document.addEventListener("DOMContentLoaded",function(){
    main();
});
```

Real-Time Data Visualization of the Gait Parameters (Patterns) on the Browser

We have a function to draw detected points on the image. We saved all the results from the PoseNet output in the poses array. Here, we loop through every pose of the person in the image and get its keypoints:

```
function gotPoses(poses)
{
    if(poses.length > 0)
    {
        pose = poses[0]
    }
}
```

We loop through every point that is a body part in the keypoints array, which further has the following:

- *Part*: The name of the part that was detected

- *Position*: x and y values of a point on the image

- *Score*: Accuracy of detection

We only draw a point with fill (red, green, blue), taking an RGB intensity value ranging from 0 to 255 to decide the color of a point:

```
function drawPoint(x, y, radius, color)
{
    ctx.beginPath();
    ctx.arc(x, y, radius, 0, 2 * Math.PI);
    ctx.fillStyle = color;
    ctx.fill();
}

function drawLine(x1,y1,x2,y2,color)
{
    ctx.beginPath();
    ctx.moveTo(x1, y1);
    ctx.lineTo(x2, y2);
    ctx.strokeStyle = color;
    ctx.lineWidth = 2;
    ctx.stroke();
}

//Similarly, the function initializeParameters do //adjust the
confidence values

async function initializeParameters(button)
{
    let eyeL = pose.pose.leftEye
    let eyeR = pose.pose.rightEye
    let ankleL = pose.pose.leftAnkle
    let ankleR = pose.pose.rightAnkle
    let count =0;
    let timeFrame = 1000
    let start = new Date().getTime();
    let end = start;
```

```
    while(end - start < timeFrame)
    {
        if(eyeL.confidence >= cnfThreshold && eyeR.confidence
        >= cnfThreshold && ankleL.confidence >= cnfThreshold &&
        ankleR.confidence>=cnfThreshold)
        {
            height_px = height_px+ (distance(0, eyeL.y, 0,
            ankleL.y) + distance(0, eyeR.y, 0, ankleR.y))/2
            start_point = start_point+ (ankleL.y +ankleR.y)/2
            lr_step_threshold = lr_step_threshold + distance(0,
            ankleL.y, 0, ankleR.y)
            count = count +1;
            button.innerHTML = "Initializing ...."
        }

        end = new Date().getTime();
    }

    height_cm = document.getElementById("height").value;
    height_px  = (height_px / count).toFixed(2);
    lr_step_threshold = ((lr_step_threshold/count) * (height_cm
/ height_px)).toFixed(2)
    start_point = (start_point / count).toFixed(2)

    button.innerHTML = "Done"
}
function toggleDistance(button)
{
    if (dflag)
    {
        dflag = false;
        button.innerHTML= "Start";
    }
```

```
    else
    {
        dflag = true;
        timer()
        button.innerHTML= "Stop";
    }
}
function timer()
{
    let sec=0,min=0;
    var time = setInterval(function(){
      if (!dflag) {
            clearInterval(time);
        }
document.getElementById('time').innerHTML=min+":"+sec;
        sec++;
        if(sec == 60)
        {
            sec=0;
            min++;
        }

    }, 1000);
}
function toggleKnee(button)
{
    if (kflag)
    {
        kflag = false;
        button.innerHTML= "Detect";
    }
```

```
    else
    {
       kflag = true;
        button.innerHTML= "Pause";
    }
}
function toggleStrideLength(button)
{
    if (strideflag)
    {
        strideflag = false;
        button.innerHTML= "Detect";
    }
    else {

        if(!rsflag){
document.getElementById("stride").innerHTML= "Activate Right
Step Length"
        }
        else if(!lsflag){
document.getElementById("stride").innerHTML = "Activate Left
Step Length"
        }
        else{
            strideflag = true;
            button.innerHTML= "Pause";
        }
    }
}
function toggleRightStep(button)
{
    if (rsflag)
```

```
    {
        rsflag = false;
        button.innerHTML= "Detect";
    }
    else
    {
        rsflag = true;
        button.innerHTML= "Pause";
    }
}

function toggleLeftStep(button)
{
    if (lsflag)
    {
        lsflag = false;
        button.innerHTML= "Detect";
    }
    else
    {
        lsflag = true;
        button.innerHTML= "Pause";
    }
}
function distance(x1,y1,x2,y2)
{
    let a = x2-x1;
    let b = y2-y1;
    let result = Math.sqrt( a*a + b*b);
    return result;
}
```

Figure 5-4 shows the initial parameters screen before entering the height of the person.

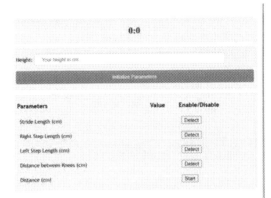

Figure 5-4. *Initial output as seen on the browser. The user has to provide the height manually (input) into the user interface and click the Detect buttons to measure the parameters*

Figure 5-5 shows the output after we enter the height of the user (in centimeters), click the Initialize Parameters button, and then click the Detect button for stride length.

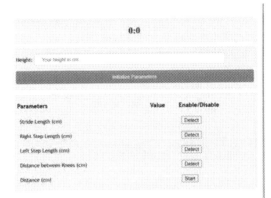

Figure 5-5. *Stride length values display after the corresponding button is clicked*

When the user clicks Right Step Length and Left Step Length buttons, the values display as shown in Figure 5-6.

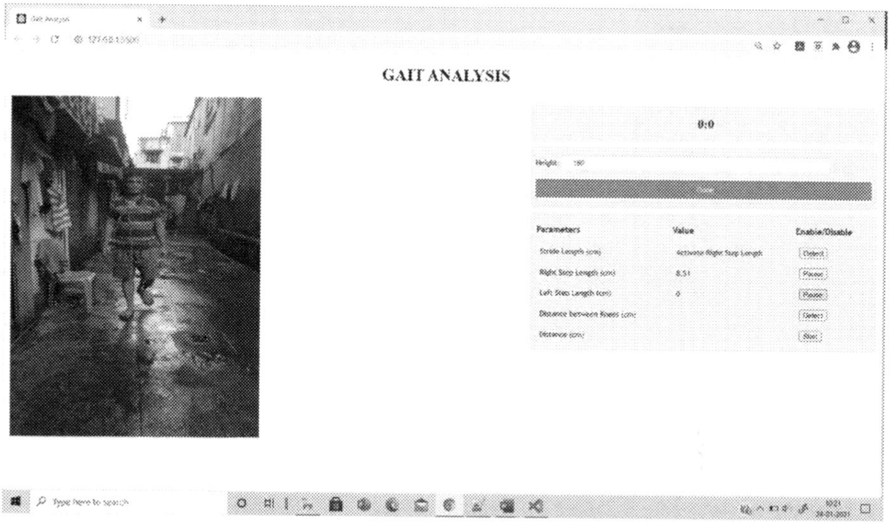

Figure 5-6. *Right step length and left step length values display after the user clicks the buttons*

The total distance covered while walking displays upon click of the Distance button, as shown in Figure 5-7.

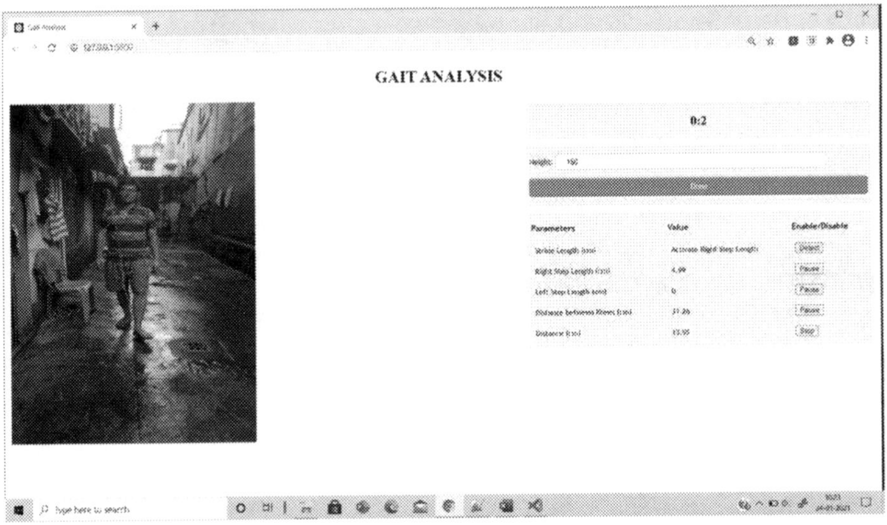

Figure 5-7. Gait parameters displayed on the web browser

Determining Gait Patterns Using Threshold Values

The threshold score in the options variable can be set to a certain value so that the corresponding poses with the scores above the threshold values display:

```
const options = {
  imageScaleFactor: 0.3,outputStride: 16,
  flipHorizontal: false,minConfidence: 0.5,
  maxPoseDetections: 2,scoreThreshold: 0.5,
  nmsRadius: 20,detectionType: 'multiple',
  multiplier: 0.75,
 }
while(end - start < timeFrame)
{
if(eyeL.confidence >= cnfThreshold && eyeR.confidence >=
cnfThreshold && ankleL.confidence >= cnfThreshold && ankleR.
confidence>=cnfThreshold)
```

160

```
{
height_px = height_px+ (distance(0, eyeL.y, 0, ankleL.y) +
distance(0, eyeR.y, 0, ankleR.y))/2
start_point = start_point+ (ankleL.y +ankleR.y)/2
            lr_step_threshold = lr_step_threshold + distance(0,
            ankleL.y, 0, ankleR.y)
            count = count +1;
            button.innerHTML = "Initializing ...."
 }
end = new Date().getTime();
}
height_cm = document.getElementById("height").value;
height_px  = (height_px / count).toFixed(2);
lr_step_threshold = ((lr_step_threshold/count) * (height_cm /
height_px)).toFixed(2)
start_point = (start_point / count).toFixed(2)
button.innerHTML = "Done"
```

Summary

Deep neural nets for stride and stance (gait) examination is a progressive thought. These measurements help assess stride irregularities, which may quantitatively indicate the proportion of medical condition seriousness that is influencing walk and stance. The measurements will help assess disturbances in gait, locomotion, balance, and risk for falls. The present methodology using AI in the browser will help with the following:

- Determining need for assistive, adaptive, orthotic, protective, supportive, or prosthetic devices or equipment

- Assessment of difficulty in integrating sensory, motor, and neural processes

- Establishing a diagnosis, prognosis, plan of care, referral to other services

- Foot Switch Stride Analysis

- Define temporal and distance factors, classify patient's ability to walk

- Measure response to treatment programs, calculation of velocity, stride length, cadence, single stance, initial and terminal double stance, total stance, gait cycle duration.

Readers of this book will develop applications such as gait analysis as described in this chapter by implementing the features learned from Chapters 1 through 4. The main features and tools to be considered in the gait analysis application's design and development are JS, DOM, jQuery, p5.js, ml5.js, and TensorFlow.js.

References

Levine D. F., J. Richards, and M. Whittle. *Whittle's Gait Analysis*. Elsevier Health Sciences, 2012.

https://en.wikipedia.org/wiki/Gait_analysis

Humphrey, Ellen, and Jim Patton. "'Normal' Gait – Part of Kinesiology." Department of Physical Therapy & Human Movement Sciences, Northwestern University, Medical School.

https://www.medicine.missouri.edu/sites/default/files/Normal-Gait-ilovepdf-compressed.pdf

Normal Gait, Heikki Uustal, MD, Medical Director, Prosthetic/Orthotic Team, JFK-Johnson Rehab Institute, Edison, NJ

CHAPTER 6

Future Possibilities for Running AI Methods in a Browser

This chapter covers two new JavaScript (JS) libraries that run with the help of the TensorFlow.js framework: face-api.js and handpose. The evolving JS libraries show a path to explore real-time responsive applications that can run on browser and computational resource devices (electronic devices with less computing capability).

Introduction

As discussed in the previous chapters, human posture assessment differs from other basic computer vision undertakings in some significant ways. Object identification finds objects inside of a picture. However, this is ordinarily coarse grained, consisting of a jumping box incorporating the object. Posture assessment goes further, foreseeing the exact area of keypoints related to the human subject.

© Nagender Kumar Suryadevara 2021
N. K. Suryadevara, *Beginning Machine Learning in the Browser*,
https://doi.org/10.1007/978-1-4842-6843-8_6

Essentially, two-dimensional (2D) assessment gauges the area of keypoints in 2D space comparative with a picture or video outline. The model gauges an x and y coordinate for each keypoint of the human being. Three-dimensional (3D) assessment attempts to change an object in a 2D picture into a 3D object by adding a z coordinate to the forecast.

3D assessment enables us to anticipate the genuine spatial situating of an individual or item. As you might expect, 3D assessment is currently a testing issue for machine learning (ML) students, given the multifaceted nature required to make datasets and calculations that consider an assortment of variables for a picture's or video's experience scene or the lighting conditions.

A qualification applies between recognizing one or various areas in a picture or video. The 2D and 3D methodologies can be alluded to as single-person and multiperson assessment. Single-person assessment approaches distinguish and track one individual or item, whereas multiperson assessment approaches recognize and track numerous individuals or items.

We can plainly imagine the intensity of posture assessment by thinking about its application in various aspects: from virtual game mentors and artificial intelligence (AI)-fueled fitness coaches to following developments on manufacturing plant floors to guaranteeing worker well-being. Current PoseNet assessment may result in a deluge of robotized devices intended to gauge human development accuracy.

The PoseNet assessment methods open up applications in the scope of zones (for example, increased reality, liveliness, gaming, and mechanical technology). This is not a thorough rundown, but it remembers a portion of the essential ways for which present assessment is forming our future.

TensorFlow.js has empowered ML analysts to make their calculations more available to other people. For instance, the Magenta.js library (Roberts et al., 2018) gave in-program admittance to generative music models created by the Magenta group and ported to the web with TensorFlow.js. Magenta.js has expanded the permeability of their work with their intended interest group (specifically, performers). This has released a wide assortment of ML-fueled music applications worked by the network. Examples include Latent Cycles Parviainen (2018a). and Neural Drum Machine Parviainen (2018b). You can find these and more models at `https://magenta.tensorflow.org/demos`.

A fundamental specialized commitment of TensorFlow.js is the arrangement of methods used to repurpose web stage design application programming interfaces (APIs) for superior numeric processing while at the same time keeping up similarity with an enormous number of gadgets and execution conditions.

We accept there are various chances to expand and upgrade TensorFlow.js. Given the fast advancement of program improvement, it appears likely that extra GPU programming models may open up. Specifically, program developers see discussions to execute broadly useful GPU programming APIs Apple (2017) W3C (2017) that will make these sorts of toolboxes more performant and simpler to maintain. Future work will zero in on improving execution, progress on gadget similarity (especially cell phones), and expand equality with the Python TensorFlow usage. We additionally observe a need to offer help for full AI work processes, including information, yield, and change.

Additional Machine Learning Applications with TensorFlow

The remaining sections discuss AI applications that can run on the browser with the help of various JS libraries.

Face Recognition Using face-api.js

Face detection and facial recognition using ML with TensorFlow in the browser. The face-api.js JS module executes convolutional neural networks (CNNs) to detect faces and recognize face marks (keypoints). The face-api.js uses TensorFlow.js and is streamlined for the work area and portable web.

In addition to face detection and recognition, a few models are available with face-api.js that enable facial expression recognition, age assessment of an individual, and gender determination.

To begin with face-api.js, web developers include the most recent JS library of face-api.js or install it using npm. The face-api.js is open-source software accessible through the MIT license.

The visualization of face detection and face marks (keypoints) using face-api.js can be viewed on the browser, as shown in Figure 6-1.

Figure 6-1. *Visualizing the detection results by drawing the bounding boxes into a canvas using the face-api.js library*

The application has two files: index1.html (Listing 6-1) and main.js , which you can download from https://justadudewhohacks.github.io/ face-api.js/docs/index.html.

Listing 6-1. Index1.html

```
<!DOCTYPE html>
<html lang="en">
  <head>
    <meta charset="UTF-8" />
    <meta name="viewport" content="width=device-width,
    initial-scale=1.0" />
    <title>AI in Browser-Face Mask Detection</title>
    </head>
  <body>
    <h1>Deep Learning in Browser-Face Mask detection for IoT/
    mOBILE Devices</h1><br><br>
    <p id="GFG"></p>
    <video id="video" height="320" width="240" autoplay true>
    </video>
    <script src="js/face-api.min.js"></script>
    <script src="js/main.js"></script>
  </body>
</html>
```

Hand Pose Estimation

Being able to see the shape and movement of hands can help to improve the client experience over an assortment of innovative areas and stages. For instance, it can shape the reason for gesture-based communication comprehension and hand signal control and likewise empower the overlay of advanced substance and data on the physical world's head in increased reality. While falling into place without any issues for individuals, robust constant hand recognition is a distinctly testing computer vision task, because hands regularly impede themselves or one another (for example, finger/palm impediments and handshakes) and need high-difference designs.

This engineering is like that utilized by us as of late distributed face work ML pipeline and that others have utilized for present assessment. Giving the precisely trimmed palm picture to the hand milestone model diminishes the requirement for information enlargement (for example, rotation, interpretation, and scaling) and rather permits the organization to commit the vast majority of its ability to facilitate expectation precision.

The hand pose estimation method determines the joints (keypoints) when the palm image or a video is given as input. Basically, the sign language precision can be easily understood from the hand pose estimation.

Figure 6-2 shows the screenshot (output) after running an AI program in the browser.

Figure 6-2. *Hand pose estimation with the keypoints*

We intend to broaden this innovation with a more stable and robust following, extend the measure of hand signals. Novel applications can be explored with the help of Hand pose estimation and we eager to see what best can be resulted from the usage of the method.

Listings 6-2 and 6-3 provide the source code (index2.html and script.js) for the hand pose estimation.

Listing 6-2. Index2.html

```
<!DOCTYPE html>
<html>
    <head>
        <title>Hand Pose Detection</title>
        <script src="https://cdn.jsdelivr.net/npm/@
        tensorflow/tfjs-core@2.4.0/dist/tf-core.min.js">
        </script>
        <script src="https://cdn.jsdelivr.net/npm/@
        tensorflow/tfjs-converter@2.4.0/dist/tf-converter.
        min.js"></script>
        <script src="https://cdn.jsdelivr.net/npm/@
        tensorflow/tfjs-backend-webgl@2.4.0/dist/tf-
        backend-webgl.min.js"></script>
        <script src="https://cdn.jsdelivr.net/npm/@
        tensorflow-models/handpose@0.0.6/dist/handpose.min.
        js"></script>
        <script src="script.js"></script>
        <style>
            #pose-canvas{
                position: absolute;
                top: 0;
                left: 0;
            }
        </style>
    </head>
    <body>
        <div id="video-container">
            <video id="pose-video" autoplay="true">
            </video>
            <canvas id="pose-canvas"></canvas>
```

```
            </div>
        </body>
</html>
```

Listing 6-3. script.js

```
const config ={
        video:{ width: 640, height: 480, fps: 50}
    };
function drawPoint(ctx, x, y, radius, color)
{
    ctx.beginPath();
    ctx.arc(x, y, radius, 0, 2 * Math.PI);
    ctx.fillStyle = color;
    ctx.fill();
}

function drawLine(ctx,x1,y1,x2,y2,color)
{
    ctx.beginPath();
    ctx.moveTo(x1, y1);
    ctx.lineTo(x2, y2);
    ctx.strokeStyle = color;
    ctx.stroke();
}

function draw(ctx,part,radius,color)
{
    let k=0;

    for(k=0; k<part.length-1; k++)
    {
        const[x1,y1,z1] = part[k];
        const[x2,y2,z2] = part[k+1];
```

```
        drawPoint(ctx,x1,y1, radius,color);
        drawLine(ctx,x1,y1,x2,y2,color);
    }

    const[x1,y1,z1] = part[k];
    drawPoint(ctx,x1,y1, radius, 0, 2 * Math.PI);
}

async function estimateHands(video, model, ctx)
{
    ctx.clearRect(0, 0, conFigure video.width, conFigure
    video.height);
    const predictions = await model.estimateHands(video);

    if (predictions.length > 0)
    {

      for(let i=0; i<predictions.length;i++)
      {
          const thumb_finger = predictions[i].
          annotations['thumb'];
          const index_finger = predictions[i].
          annotations['indexFinger'];
          const middle_finger = predictions[i].
          annotations['middleFinger'];
          const ring_finger = predictions[i].
          annotations['ringFinger'];
          const pinky_finger = predictions[i].
          annotations['pinky'];
          const palm = predictions[i].annotations['palmBase'];

          draw(ctx,thumb_finger,3,'red');
          draw(ctx,index_finger,3,'red');
          draw(ctx,middle_finger,3,'red');
```

```
        draw(ctx,ring_finger,3,'red');
        draw(ctx,pinky_finger,3,'red');

        let[x1,y1,z1] = palm[0];
        drawPoint(ctx,x1,y1, 3, 0, 2 * Math.PI);

        let[x2,y2,z2] = thumb_finger[0];
        drawLine(ctx,x1,y1,x2,y2,'red');

        [x2,y2,z2] = index_finger[0];
        drawLine(ctx,x1,y1,x2,y2,'red');

        [x2,y2,z2] = middle_finger[0];
        drawLine(ctx,x1,y1,x2,y2,'red');

        [x2,y2,z2] = ring_finger[0];
        drawLine(ctx,x1,y1,x2,y2,'red');

        [x2,y2,z2] = pinky_finger[0];
        drawLine(ctx,x1,y1,x2,y2,'red');

      }
    }
    setTimeout(function(){
      estimateHands(video, model, ctx);
    }, 1000 / conFigure video.fps)
}

async function main()
{
    const video = document.getElementById("pose-video");
    const model = await handpose.load();
    const canvas =  document.getElementById("pose-canvas");
```

```
    const ctx = canvas.getContext("2d");
      estimateHands(video, model,ctx);
      console.log("Starting predictions")
}

async function init_camera()
{
    const constraints ={
      audio: false,
      video:{
      width: conFigure video.width,
      height: conFigure video.height,
      frameRate: { max: conFigure video.fps }
      }
    };

    const video = document.getElementById("pose-video");
    video.width = conFigure video.width;
    video.height= conFigure video.height;

navigator.mediaDevices.getUserMedia(constraints).then(stream => {
      video.srcObject = stream;
        main();
    });
}

function init_canvas()
{
      const canvas =  document.getElementById("pose-canvas");
      canvas.width = conFigure video.width;
      canvas.height = conFigure video.height;
      console.log("Canvas initialized");
}
```

```
document.addEventListener('DOMContentLoaded',function(){
  init_canvas();
  init_camera();
});
```

Following are the parameters for the handpose.load in the async function:

Parameters for handpose.load()

handpose.load() takes a configuration object with the following properties:

- **maxContinuousChecks** - How many frames to go without running the bounding box detector. Defaults to infinity. Set to a lower value if you want a safety net in case the mesh detector produces consistently flawed predictions.

- **detectionConfidence** - Threshold for discarding a prediction. Defaults to 0.8.

- **iouThreshold** - A float representing the threshold for deciding whether boxes overlap too much in non-maximum suppression. Must be between [0, 1]. Defaults to 0.3.

- **scoreThreshold** - A threshold for deciding when to remove boxes based on score in non-maximum suppression. Defaults to 0.75.

Parameters for handpose.estimateHands()

- **input** - The image to classify. Can be a tensor, DOM element image, video, or canvas.

- **flipHorizontal** - Whether to flip/mirror the facial keypoints horizontally. Should be true for videos that are flipped by default (e.g. webcams).

Summary

TensorFlow.js enables web developers to prepare and run AI models entirely in their browsers or resource-constrained devices. It is an great way for JS developers to discover advances in the universe of AI. The best thing is not normal for CoreML, which runs inside Apple's environment. TensorFlow.js can run on iOS, macOS, Linux, Android, and any stage that support a program.

I trust the libraries mentioned in this chapter motivate you to begin building astonishing AI-fueled web applications.

References

https://justadudewhohacks.github.io/face-api.js/docs/index.html

https://glitch.com/~face-api-js-for-beginners

https://github.com/tensorflow/tfjs-models/tree/master/handpose

https://blog.tensorflow.org/2020/03/face-and-hand-tracking-in-browser-with-mediapipe-and-tensorflowjs.html

A. Roberts, C. Hawthorne and I. Simon, "Magenta.js: A JavaScript API for Augmenting Creativity with Deep Learning." 2018 Joint Workshop on Machine Learning for Music (ICML).

Conclusion

AI is becoming ubiquitous, a part of our everyday lives, especially in computer browsers and myriad electronic devices. Applying AI methods through browser has many advantages. Running AI in the browser can accelerate computing activities by executing them legitimately at the client end itself. It can execute with the help of API methods at the client side rather than via cloud computing methods.

It can likewise provide an AI app that can collect rich information from customer mobile device sensors such as webcams, amplifiers, and GPS. It tends to provide privacy by running browser-based AI information at the customer end. Also, it brings AI close enough for the immense pool of web developers who work in JS and other client-side dialects, structures, and devices.

The browser-side programming languages and scripts help demonstrate, prepare, execute, and represent AI, interactive learning, and other AI models in the program. They would all be able to take advantage of privately introduced designs preparing units and other AI-improved equipment to speed model execution. In addition, many of them give built-in and pretrained neural net models to speed improvement of relapse, order, picture acknowledgment, and other AI-empowered tasks in the browser.

AI in-browser applications are proliferating. Google has the most tools to help web developers construct ML and DL applications for the browser and to develop customer applications and gadgets.

Google expanding the TensorFlow framework, an intuitive representation of neural networks written in TypeScript. This new framework supports intelligent JS improvements of customer-side AI applications in which models are assembled and prepared completely or generally in the browser, with their information staying there. It likewise permits pretrained AI models to be imported—or changed through transfer learning—just for program-based inferencing. The system enables designers to import models recently prepared disconnected in Python with Keras or TensorFlow SavedModels and afterward use them for inferencing or move learning in the program, utilizing WebGL quickening for client-side GPU acceleration. The TensorFlow.js group is intending to refresh it to help the back-end Node.js JS advancement system, as follows:

- *Mobile device embedded AI system*: Google officially delivered Swift for TensorFlow and made this open-source ML advancement structure accessible on GitHub. The developed system by the Google can be useful across multiple platforms.

- *Updates to its mobile computer vision AI library*: The organization presented MobileNetV2, the most recent age group of broadly useful, DL-fueled computer vision neural organizations inserted in cell phones.

- *Updates to its broadly useful, electronic gadget-implanted AI structure*: Google latest releases include the Tensorflow lite, a lightweight framework which converts the prepared ML model into an versatile program to run on the edge devices. The edge device such as Raspberry Pi can easily execute the ML models efficiently.

Index

© Nagender Kumar Suryadevara 2021
N. K. Suryadevara, *Beginning Machine Learning in the Browser*,
https://doi.org/10.1007/978-1-4842-6843-8

Printed in the United States
by Baker & Taylor Publisher Services